Praise for *Meet Every Lea*

"This is the best book I have ever read on classroom instructional delivery. Every teacher should understand these methods and techniques!"
—**Rex Bolinger**, EdD, former Indiana High School Principal of the Year and National Milken Educator

"Every parent and educator I know is continuously thinking about how we can modernize classroom instruction and make it more effective and interesting for our students. Robert Barnett's book is a road map toward how we can rethink our classrooms while building a love of teaching and learning. If you are a teacher thinking about ways to make a difference, this book is for you."
—**James Lane**, CEO of PDK International

"Whether you're a classroom teacher or a school or system leader, you've been tasked with what can often feel like an impossible mission. Fortunately, *Meet Every Learner's Needs* equips you with a practical toolkit to transform both what you do and how you do it. You'll discover strategies to maximize your skills, time, and relationships with students, while minimizing frustration—ultimately leading to deeper student engagement and learning."
—**Deborah Gist**, former district superintendent and state education commissioner

"The Modern Classrooms Project is a breakthrough education model that leverages the power of technology in the classroom while honoring—and amplifying—the authentic teacher-student relationship that is always at the heart of both student success and teacher satisfaction. *Meet Every Learner's Needs* is a remarkable primer on how the Modern Classrooms Project model works to transform classrooms, students, and teachers by focusing on efficacy and equity to ensure all students succeed and by empowering teachers to stay and thrive in the profession. This book should be widely read by both educators looking to meet the learning needs of all of their students and by education policy makers seeking innovations that work and should be replicated nationwide."

—**Michael Brown**, co-founder of City Year and principal of Public Purpose Strategies

"Meeting the needs of every student has been a challenge for teachers forever, and the Modern Classrooms Project approach may finally have a solution that really works. Barnett's practical and inspiring book explains how any teacher, in any school, can redesign instruction to ensure that every student achieves their potential. This method has worked for educators around the world, and with the help of this guide, it can work for you too."

—**Jennifer Gonzalez**, editor-in-chief of *Cult of Pedagogy*

"Barnett describes in detail an approach to the Modern Classrooms Project teaching model, which is mind-blowing but well worth the time of an educator who wants to get better. He explains how to accelerate *every* student, from wherever they are and at a pace they can handle, a method that has never occurred to me in the 40 years I have been writing about teachers but—startling to me—makes great sense."

—**Jay Mathews**, education columnist of the *Washington Post*

"Fully customizing instruction is a near impossibility in traditional classroom models. Yet with a different instructional design, so much more is possible—for students and educators alike. This book provides an essential blueprint for making that shift at the classroom level. It is essential reading for educators everywhere."

—**Jeff Wetzler**, co-founder of Transcend, former chief learning officer of Teach for America, and author of *Ask: Tap Into the Hidden Wisdom of People Around You*

"*Meet Every Learner's Needs* is equal parts inspiration and revelation. It tells the win-win story of how self-paced learning turns children onto achieving and helps disenchanted educators rediscover why they were drawn to teaching."

—**Hugh B. Price**, former president and CEO of National Urban League and author of *Achievement Matters: Getting Your Child the Best Education Possible*

Meet Every Learner's Needs

Meet Every Learner's Needs

Redesigning Instruction So All Students Can Succeed

Robert Barnett

FOREWORD BY **Kareem Farah,**
Co-Founder and CEO of the Modern Classrooms Project

JB JOSSEY-BASS™
A Wiley Brand

Jossey-Bass, a Wiley imprint

Published by John Wiley & Sons, Inc., Hoboken, New Jersey.

Published simultaneously in Canada.

For general information on our other products and services, please contact our Customer Care Department within the United States at (800) 762-2974, outside the United States at (317) 572-3993. For product technical support, you can find answers to frequently asked questions or reach us via live chat at https://support.wiley.com.

If you believe you've found a mistake in this book, please bring it to our attention by emailing our reader support team at wileysupport@wiley.com with the subject line "Possible Book Errata Submission."

Wiley also publishes its books in a variety of electronic formats. Some content that appears in print may not be available in electronic formats. For more information about Wiley products, visit our website at www.wiley.com.

Library of Congress Cataloging-in-Publication Data

Names: Barnett, Robert, author.
Title: Meet every learner's needs : redesigning instruction so all students
    can succeed / Robert Barnett.
Description: Hoboken, New Jersey : Jossey-Bass, [2025] | Includes index.
Identifiers: LCCN 2024036887 (print) | LCCN 2024036888 (ebook) | ISBN
    9781394274895 (Paperback) | ISBN 9781394274918 (adobe pdf) | ISBN
    9781394274901 (epub)
Subjects: LCSH: Effective teaching. | Academic achievement.
Classification: LCC LB1025.3 .B3564 2025 (print) | LCC LB1025.3 (ebook) |
    DDC 371.102—dc23/eng/20240913
LC record available at https://lccn.loc.gov/2024036887
LC ebook record available at https://lccn.loc.gov/2024036888

Cover Design: Wiley
Cover Image: © SIBGHA /Adobe Stock

SKY10094564_122624

To my sons Joshua and Simon, and my niece Winnie—
I've written this book because it describes the kind of education
I hope you, and every member of your generation, will receive.

Contents

Teacher Tips

Acknowledgments

I knew writing a book would be hard work for me. I didn't realize how much others would contribute!

Amanda von Moos, Jay Mathews, and Michael Brown encouraged me to go for it. Ashante Thomas saw the potential in the book and—more importantly—saw the process the whole way through. Felipe Martinez, Kris Subhash, Megan McGregor, Paul Magnuson, Sarah Burkett, Sean Hamidi, Shant'l Olovson, and Torre' Mills read messy drafts and shared clear feedback. Kim Wimpsett provided keen insight, detailed edits, and much-needed reassurance. Jasmine Brooks helped make the cover beautiful. If you ever need advice on a book deal, ask Ian Polonsky.

This book represents my life's work to date, and writing it has given me a lens to reflect on both. Life first: as with everything good in my world, Melinda Kuritzky's love and support made writing this book possible—and reading it (I hope) reasonably interesting. I asked for her advice often, and she was almost always right. I wrote most of this book early in the mornings, before my sons Joshua and Simon woke up, and I always knew that no matter how well or poorly the morning's writing had gone, I'd be glad when they did. They are all the inspiration I could ever need.

Luckily, I have other sources too. My parents Iris and Phil inspire me to read, write, and do good, then believe in me every step of the way. My sister Nora is an amazing educator and my sister Eve an amazing editor: I aspire to be like each of them in countless ways. My grandparents, in-laws, uncles, and aunts—including Kitty who offered me her writer's ear and Rena who shared her designer's eye—make me feel like I can do anything. My friends are always there for me. And we've all had a lot of fun over the years.

Like many educators, I went into teaching because of the many wonderful people who taught me. From my first day of pre-kindergarten to my last semester of graduate school, I was lucky to learn from teachers who challenged me, supported me, and above all cared about the person I would become. They passed up easier and higher-paying jobs to help me and my classmates grow. The highest compliment I can pay them is that I decided to become a teacher too.

When I did—first at Aki Kurose Middle School in Seattle, then at Maret School and Eastern Senior High School in Washington, DC, and finally at Leysin American School and École CREA Genève in Switzerland—I was surrounded by extraordinary peers. I pestered them with questions, and they responded with wisdom and compassion. I succeeded as a teacher because of the example they set, and still count many of them as role models, mentors, and friends.

And when I considered leaving the classroom, Shane Donovan showed me that a better way was possible. Nick Bennett and Matt Kennedy helped me figure out how. Rachel Skerritt, Sah Brown, and Marc Ott trusted me to do my thing. Déson Hall and Lucas Cooke pushed me to work through the kinks. Justin Sybenga guided me to find my voice.

I loved teaching. My colleague Kareem Farah did too. But he convinced me that the approach we had developed—an instructional model that meets every learner's needs—was worth sharing with the world, and I will forever be grateful that he did. We co-founded the Modern Classrooms Project (MCP) in 2018 and have empowered many thousands of teachers together in the years since. Kareem's charisma, vision, and tenacity power everything that MCP does. I feel fortunate to know him, and to work alongside him in service of learners and educators everywhere.

I also feel fortunate to work alongside my colleagues at MCP. Joining a young, scrappy nonprofit requires a leap of faith, and MCP in its current form exists only because so many incredibly talented people have taken that leap. It is an honor to wake up every day and watch our diverse, devoted, and diligent team make this world a better place, one classroom at a time. Our staff members—past, present, and future—propel our movement forward, and I can't wait to see where they lead us next.

That future, in turn, depends on a vast network of generous individuals whose contributions give MCP life. Our donors give us their hard-earned money. Our advisors give us their insight and wisdom. Our school and district partners give us the opportunity to support their teachers, and those teachers give us their precious time. I hope every person who has invested their energy or resources in MCP knows how grateful I am. And despite everything we have achieved together, I still feel like we're just getting started.

Of course, neither my career nor MCP would have evolved in the first place without the grace, adaptability, and honesty of my students. They tolerated my experiments, trusted me enough to follow my lead, and told me in no uncertain terms when something didn't work. I think of them every single day. I hope this book does justice to both their infinite potential and their infinitely diverse needs.

If there's a theme here, it's that I have many more people to thank—teachers, colleagues, contributors, students—than I can possibly name here. What an immense privilege that is.

Finally, and perhaps most importantly—because now you can join our band of pragmatic idealists, and help us advance this vital work—I want to thank you for reading this book.

I hope it helps you succeed.

About the Author

Robert Barnett lives with his wife and children in his hometown of Washington, DC, close to family and lifelong friends. He taught math, computer science, English, social studies, and law, from the middle-school to university levels, at public and private schools in the United States and Switzerland, and co-founded the Modern Classrooms Project with Kareem Farah in 2018. He speaks English, French, and Spanish; served as a City Year corps member; and enjoys riddles and silly jokes.

You can learn more about Robert and his work at rsbarnett.com.

Foreword

In August 2016, I began my fourth year teaching. I was in a new school in a new district, and I was struggling.

Like many educators, I had a tortured relationship with my career. Part of me was enamored with teaching. It was an exciting and dynamic profession that filled me with purpose. But it was challenging. In fact, it was the most challenging thing I have ever done. I took the right steps, and I put in the work, but I still felt like I was fighting a battle I could never win.

If you are a current or former educator reading this, you know what I am talking about. If you have never led a classroom, just know that the task at hand feels unconquerable. You walk into the building and receive a classroom, a daily schedule, a rigorous curriculum to follow, a detailed pacing calendar that tells you what to teach every day, and a roster of students whose needs are incredibly diverse. In each of my Algebra 2 classes that year, I had students testing at a third-grade level in math and students testing at a college level. Those students sat right beside each other as I delivered my lessons.

A few months into the school year, I began to reach a breaking point. I was teaching like I had been taught to teach: I stood at the front of the room and explained something new, gave my students an assignment to work on, assessed them at the end of each class, and moved on to the next thing the next day. This wasn't working. My assessments revealed that a small fraction of students actually understood my content, but I had to move on anyway. (Or so I thought.) I wasn't meeting my students' needs, and they were growing increasingly frustrated.

I didn't know how much longer I could continue doing something that felt so ineffective. It was likely going to be my last year in the classroom.

Things all changed when I met Rob Barnett. It was an ordinary weekday, and the math teachers at Eastern Senior High School gathered for our weekly meeting before classes started. I was burning out, and already eager for the day to end, when I noticed Rob sitting at a desk, alarmingly calm, working on a math problem. I had a sense at the time that he had figured something out, that he had found a pathway to teaching that didn't leave him perpetually stressed but instead allowed him to feel true joy for the profession.

I was right. Rob did figure something out. He had built his version of what we now call the Modern Classroom instructional model, and it was having a transformative impact.

Shortly after that meeting, Rob invited me to his classroom. What I saw there was magical. He had fundamentally restructured how learning happened, so that his and his students' time would be optimized. Students led the learning process, and Rob was a facilitator. Students were collaborating with each other and mastering content. Nobody seemed stressed.

What was so fascinating was that Rob did this with the same tools and materials I had. To do what Rob was doing, I didn't need to invest in a bunch of new stuff—I just needed to rethink how I used my existing resources. That meant I could go home that night and begin my own journey of transforming my classroom.

Rob also had—and still has—a generous spirit. He genuinely wanted to help me find a better way to teach. He gave me his time and resources, then welcomed me into his classroom so I could see his ideas in action and adapt them into my own. It was my first real example of authentic collaboration. We shared feedback and advice freely, with an understanding that we had one common goal: to improve our students' learning experiences. It reinvigorated my passion for teaching.

I get filled with joy knowing that you will soon experience what I did years ago, when I first met Rob: an endless flow of inspirational ideas woven into a practical framework that can lead to immediate change. He will push you to challenge some of the most basic constraints that shape schooling today, but will always pair that with actionable techniques that you can deploy tomorrow. In a system full of problems and barriers, Rob will introduce you to real solutions that give you hope. Just be careful, because it might change how you think about learning for the rest of your life. It certainly did for me.

Kareem Farah
Co-Founder and CEO
Modern Classrooms Project
September 2024

Learning Objectives

By the end of this book, you will be able to:

1. Explain why traditional instruction fails to meet many learners' needs.
2. Use research-backed teaching practices to keep every student appropriately challenged—and appropriately supported—every day.
3. Lead other educators in creating classrooms where all students can succeed.

I used the practices I'll describe, which I call the *Modern Classroom instructional model*, in my own classroom. I've seen educators around the world adopt the same practices, then feel happier and more capable as a result. I want my children to learn in Modern Classrooms too.

You can implement these practices in any grade level or content area, in any school, anywhere in the world. You can and should adapt these practices to make them your own. And you can get started, with simple next steps that will save you time and stress, right away.

Thousands of teachers, in all fifty states and countries from Australia to Zambia, have taken these steps already. You'll find tips from them throughout this book. One day I hope you'll share your Modern Classroom story too.

And if there's something here that you don't think will work for you or your students, you're probably right. So take what you like and forget the rest. You know what your students need, and I trust your judgment.

But if the young people you serve need different things, and you want all of them to succeed, then I think this book can help.

Introduction:
The Fundamental
Challenge of Teaching

Do you ever struggle to…

♦ Challenge the most advanced learners in your class?

♦ Support learners with below-grade-level skills?

♦ Help chronically absent students catch up?

When I taught in the way I was trained to teach—delivering a single new lesson to all of my students every day—I struggled to do any of these things well. I spent hours preparing my lessons, then did my best to deliver them. But most of the time, my advanced students seemed bored. My students who lacked grade-level skills seemed lost. And my students who were absent missed out altogether. I was working as hard as I could, but it always felt like there were students I just couldn't reach.

This was exhausting—and disheartening. My job was to help every learner succeed. Every day, I fell short.

No matter what I did, my lessons always seemed too easy for some students and too hard for others. I tried desperately to keep my students engaged, but they all needed different things—and there was just one of me. Each day that I failed to challenge the students who were ahead, or to support those who had fallen behind, felt like a precious day wasted. And I had no idea what to do about the learners who weren't there. I loved my students, but I was miserable. I often wanted to quit.

If I was going to make it as a teacher—and help my students achieve their full potential—I needed a new approach.

So I redesigned my lessons. Rather than delivering the same content at the same time to all of my students, whether they were prepared for it or not, I explained my content using short instructional videos, then gave each learner the time they actually needed to master each new skill. That kept every student appropriately challenged—and therefore engaged—every day. It freed me up to spend class time working closely with my students. And it was fun!

Next I redesigned my courses. I let my students learn at their own paces for days at a time, and required that each student master foundational skills before accessing more advanced content. I sat down with my students, got to know them as human beings, and marveled as I saw each of them, no matter their prior knowledge, take ownership and pride in their learning.

Finally I shared this approach—now called the Modern Classroom instructional model—with my colleagues. I showed Kareem Farah, who taught downstairs from me, and we founded the Modern Classrooms Project (MCP) in order to show others. Today there are thousands of educators, all over the world, leading their own Modern Classrooms in every subject you can imagine, from kindergarten to college and beyond.

Research shows that these teachers feel happier and more effective, while their students feel more engaged and more capable. I want you to experience these benefits too, so I've written this book to share the Modern Classroom model with you. In reading it you'll discover evidence-based practices you can use right away, as well as insights from educators who use this approach in their classrooms every day.

Before you start redesigning instruction, however, there are four realities you should understand.

Reality #1: Teaching Is Really Hard

I didn't realize how hard teaching could be until my first week at Eastern Senior High School.

The week started off well enough. I had a few years of teaching experience by that point—I had worked as a classroom aide and taught at a small independent school—so I felt comfortable in front of a class. I found my new students intelligent, curious, and eager to succeed. I loved my content, loved working with young people, and felt excited to work in a comprehensive public high school in my hometown of Washington, DC. Teaching at Eastern was a dream.

Once I began my lessons, however, it became a nightmare. My job was to teach precalculus. Yet in every one of my classes, I had students who excelled in math, students who struggled with basic concepts like exponents and fractions, and students who rarely showed up at all. In my first-period class, for instance, I taught:

◆ **David**, who loved math and wanted to become an engineer. He knew he would study calculus in college, and he wanted to be prepared.

◆ **Anna**, whose math skills were many years below grade level—and who dreaded math as a result. Anna had failed every standardized math test she had ever taken, but she was in my class anyway. All Anna wanted was to make it through the year.

◆ **Troy**, who often missed class or showed up late. I didn't know why Troy was absent so often, but I knew he had challenges at home. Even when he was in class, Troy often seemed distracted.

I realized that if I tried to push David, I'd lose Anna. If I slowed down to support Anna, I'd bore David. And when Troy showed up after missing class, he'd inevitably be confused. I had no idea how to deliver a single lesson that could meaningfully engage these three learners at the same time—let alone the other twenty students in the class! So I stood at the board, feeling helpless.

I faced the fundamental challenge of teaching: every learner has different needs. David needed a challenge; Anna needed support; Troy needed to get back on track. Until I figured out how to meet all their needs at once, none of these young people could achieve their full potential. Nor, for that matter, could I.

This challenge may seem unique to math, or to large public schools like Eastern. It isn't. Knowledge in every discipline builds upon itself, so students who lack foundational skills in any subject will inevitably struggle to access grade-level content. In every school some students will inevitably learn faster than their peers; others will inevitably be late or absent. The learners in any given class, therefore, will inevitably need different things.

So I faced this challenge again at Leysin American School in Switzerland, the elite international boarding school where I taught both math and social studies after leaving Eastern. I see this challenge at play in my own children's classrooms today. In fact, I encounter the fundamental challenge of teaching everywhere I go: students like David need to be pushed, while students like Anna and Troy need help catching up. It's inevitable.

So when I speak with teachers—at least before they adopt the Modern Classroom model—I often hear the same things. No matter where or what they teach, educators tell me:

- ◆ "I don't have time to challenge my advanced students."
- ◆ "I struggle to support students whose skills are below grade level."
- ◆ "I can't teach students who aren't in class."
- ◆ "I'm doing the best I can, but it's never enough."

Maybe you've felt these things as well.

If you have, it's not your fault. Nor is it a reflection of your commitment or belief in your students. Helping *every* student succeed, in the limited amount of time you have together, is really hard! It's the fundamental challenge of teaching. And if you don't have a practical way to meet every learner's needs, it can make your job feel downright impossible.

TEACHER TIP

CHRIS GUPTON, HIGH SCHOOL SCIENCE TEACHER (FRANKLIN, TENNESSEE)

"I came to teaching from a career in the Army, where if you worked hard enough and you planned well enough, training would go smoothly. But teaching is different. No matter how hard you plan your lesson or how hard you work on setting up your room, the students have a vote in how that's going to go. And if you haven't taken into account their needs and their interests, then working hard and being smart isn't enough.

"The Modern Classroom model really helped me respond to each of my students' needs and interests, which made teaching and learning more effective and fun for all of us."

Reality #2: Our Students Are Languishing

Let's be clear about the stakes here. Teaching is a tough job, but what students learn in school shapes the courses of their lives.

Unfortunately, our school system fails to provide many learners the instruction they need. Consider David, whose education often failed to challenge him. Consider Anna, whose education often failed to support her. Or consider Troy, who often missed out altogether. When these students' classes are consistently too easy, or too hard, or inaccessible, none of them can truly succeed.

So our young people languish. They are bored, or they are lost, or they simply don't know where to begin. They spend years of their lives in classes that fail to engage them, then leave school lacking essential skills as a result. Consider that, in 2022:

- ◆ Only 36% of American fourth-graders were considered proficient in math, and just 33% were considered proficient in reading.[1]

- ◆ By eighth grade, only 26% of American students were considered proficient in math, and just 31% were considered proficient in reading.[2]

- ◆ Only 22% of American high-school graduates were considered ready for college.[3]

- ◆ 28% of American students were considered chronically absent.[4]

These statistics were influenced by the COVID-19 pandemic, but data before COVID tells the same story. A significant majority of American students have been considered below proficient for decades, and on any given day a large percentage aren't in class at all.[5]

---

[1] See National Assessment of Educational Progress. 2023. "NAEP Report Cards." Nationsreportcard.gov. 2023. www.nationsreportcard.gov.
[2] Ibid.
[3] This is the percentage of students who met all four college-readiness benchmarks on the ACT test. See "Grad Class Database 2022—ACT Research." 2024. ACT. https://www.act.org/content/act/en/research/services-and-resources/data-and-visualization.html.
[4] Chronic absenteeism is defined as the percentage of students missing at least 10% of a school year. See "Return to Learn Tracker." 2024. Return to Learn Tracker. www.returntolearntracker.net.
[5] In 2019, for instance, only 41% of American fourth-graders were considered proficient in math and just 35% were considered proficient in reading; by eighth grade, only 34% of American students were considered proficient in math and just 34% were considered proficient in reading. Only 26% of American high-school graduates were considered ready for college. And in 2018, 15% of American students were considered chronically absent. These rates are somewhat better than the post-COVID statistics from 2022, but they are still problematic.

National statistics don't say much about any individual classroom: proficiency rates vary between communities and, sadly, across predictable demographic lines. But no matter what or where you teach, I bet you know students like David, Anna, and Troy.

Every single one of those young people deserves instruction that meets their needs.

TEACHER TIP

TORRE' MILLS, HIGH SCHOOL MATH TEACHER (BLAKELY, GEORGIA)

"Even with my best efforts, I never felt like I could reach all of my students each year. So many of my students come to me with large gaps in their understanding, and I could never fully close those gaps in our time together. As an educator, that was extremely challenging for me to accept.

"Teaching in a Modern Classroom, however, has given me a renewed sense of hope and courage. I can now spend more time directly serving each student. I can clarify misconceptions, resolve confusion, and help more of my kids. I am also teaching my kids to be more independent and self-directed learners. I'm now able to close those gaps and teach valuable life skills at the same time."

Reality #3: There Is a Better Way

What teachers and students both require is a method of teaching that responds to every learner's needs. We need an instructional approach that can challenge David, support Anna, and help Troy catch up—all at the same time, and all in the same classroom.

I am happy to report that an approach like this exists. I used it myself! As I'll explain throughout this book, this approach transformed my classroom and saved my career. And I've now seen thousands of other educators, from kindergarten teachers to university professors, in all content areas and all around the globe, implement it too. At this very moment, this approach is helping young people somewhere in the world understand something new.

This approach, which I call the Modern Classroom instructional model, works like this:

1. A teacher delivers new content through short, focused videos.

2. Each student learns from these videos at their own pace, in school or at home.

3. Students work together, with support from their teacher, to apply what they've learned.

4. When each student is ready, they attempt to demonstrate mastery of the content or skills in question. If they show mastery, they advance to the next lesson; if not, they go back and revise until they are ready to try again.

Learning in a Modern Classroom is self-paced: within defined intervals, students take the time they need to master each lesson. Teachers, freed from the task of explaining new content from the front of the room, spend class time working closely with students, either one-on-one or in small groups. Every student is appropriately challenged—and appropriately supported—every day.

A few things to note here:

◆ **This approach uses technology in a limited and purposeful way.** Videos replace a small part of each lesson—the teacher's delivery of new content—and students spend most of class collaborating with their classmates and teachers off-screen. And while having one Internet-connected device per student makes this model easier to implement, it isn't necessary. I'll explain how you can make this model work with whatever technology you have.

◆ **This approach enhances equity and human connection.** While there are other instructional methods that incorporate technology, the Modern Classroom model improves upon these approaches in ways that make teaching and learning more personal, more accessible, and more engaging.

◇ Compared to fully asynchronous online courses, in which students spend hours in front of screens, Modern Classroom educators keep their videos brief so that students can spend most of class working together, face to face. In fact, the primary purpose of video instruction is to free up teacher and student time for high-quality human interaction.

◇ Compared to "flipped" classrooms, in which students watch videos at home and work together in class, Modern Classrooms don't require students to access videos at home, or to advance through content at the same pace as their peers. Students in Modern Classrooms use videos, in and/or outside of school, to achieve mastery at their own paces.

◇ While the Modern Classroom model works well for remote learning—one educator calls it "pandemic-proof"[6]—it is designed for in-person learning. In fact, the vast majority of teachers who implement it teach in traditional school settings. These educators, however, appreciate the flexibility and accessibility that this approach allows when either they or their students can't make it to class.

If anything, the Modern Classroom model is most similar to the pedagogy of the pre-industrial one-room schoolhouse: it creates learning environments in which teachers work closely with diverse groups of students, tailoring their instruction to meet every learner's actual needs.[7] Modern technology is just a tool that makes this fundamentally human pedagogy possible at scale. And the teacher is, now as then, at the heart of it all.

◆ **This approach makes teaching easier.** Running a Modern Classroom may sound like a lot of work. And it can be, especially at first: it often takes longer to find or record concise instructional videos than it does to lecture live, and developing systems to support self-paced learning requires patience and commitment.

In the long run, however, teaching in a Modern Classroom can save you a tremendous amount of time and effort. Once you have a good video, for instance, you never need to repeat

---

[6] Woodard, Montenique. "A Pandemic-Proof Approach to Teaching." Next Generation Learning Challenges, March 17, 2020. Monte is a middle-school science teacher and, if you use Facebook, her name may be familiar: Monte manages the lively "Modern Classrooms Project—Teacher Discussion" Facebook Group (https://www.facebook.com/groups/modernclassrooms), which as of September 2024 has more than 20,000 members worldwide.

[7] Ever since the nineteenth century, when Western schools largely adopted a factory-like model in which students move through standardized classes according to their age, educational thinkers such as John Dewey, Maria Montessori, and Helen Parkhurst have proposed alternatives more focused on individual learners' needs. Their thinking influenced the mastery learning movement of the late twentieth century, in which educators like Benjamin Bloom and Fred Keller designed systems that required learners to show understanding before progressing to more advanced content. It is this long pedagogical tradition, backed by decades of research on the benefits of learner-centered and/or mastery-based approaches, that informs the Modern Classroom model today.

that explanation again. And once you've stopped lecturing, you can review students' work and meet with individual learners during class, rather than waiting until after school. By my second year using this approach, teaching felt easy: I already had all my videos and systems in place, so I just showed up every day and helped my students learn.

This approach empowers teachers, supports students, and makes school more enjoyable for both. And don't just take my word for it! For three years, MCP worked with researchers at Johns Hopkins University to evaluate Modern Classrooms' impacts on both students and teachers. My analysis of the data they collected shows that Modern Classrooms help educators feel more capable and more effective (see Table I.1), while their learners feel happier and more successful (see Table I.2).[8]

TABLE I.1   Key Benefits for Teachers

STATEMENT	% AGREEMENT IN TRADITIONAL CLASSROOMS	% AGREEMENT IN MODERN CLASSROOMS
I am able to work closely with each of my students during class.	19%	86%
I feel I am able to effectively serve students at all levels of understanding.	44%	89%
I can easily help students who have missed class to catch up.	11%	100%

I'll share some of these teachers' experiences and insights, along with additional evidence of Modern Classrooms' impacts, throughout this book.

---

[8] The data in both tables comes from one of several program evaluations that MCP performed in partnership with researchers at Johns Hopkins University. For the full analysis, see Wolf, B., Eisinger, J., & Ross, S. (2020). The Modern Classrooms Project: Survey Results for the 2019–20 School Year. Baltimore, MD: Johns Hopkins University. The data in this table was collected in January 2020, before the students or teachers surveyed were affected by COVID, and all findings are statistically significant ($p < 0.001$).

TABLE I.2 Key Benefits for Students

STATEMENT	% AGREEMENT IN TRADITIONAL CLASSROOMS	% AGREEMENT IN MODERN CLASSROOMS
I am capable of learning anything.	73%	80%
I like the way my teacher teaches this class.	76%	84%
I enjoy learning.	59%	70%

Most importantly, this is an approach that you can actually use—in any grade level or content area, anywhere in the world. And if you follow the guidance in this book, as thousands of other teachers have, you can start meeting every learner's needs tomorrow.

TEACHER TIP

ERIN BLASER, K-8 STEM TEACHER (SEATTLE, WASHINGTON)

"I love creating videos because they are authentic (it's me on the videos!) and available to students whenever they are ready for it, whether that's during the unit or even after we're done. It puts the focus on understanding, so students don't rush ahead, skip through, or copy each other's work. Teaching this way has honestly changed the way I'll teach forever.

"And if you're just starting off, trust in the process! Self-pacing takes time to institute, and just like your students will have a learning curve, you will too. Creating a Modern Classroom is a self-paced adventure of its own. But it's fulfilling, rejuvenating, and exciting—and well worth the effort."

Reality #4: This Starts With You

Ultimately, I believe that individual educators can lead meaningful change—in their classrooms and beyond—because I've seen so many who have. I've seen teachers redesign individual lessons, then transform entire courses, then inspire their colleagues to do the same. I've seen many teachers do these things better than I ever did! And I've seen classrooms, schools, and communities become places where teachers are excited to teach and students are eager to learn.

So that's what I want to help you do: create a classroom, and then a world, where you and each of your students can truly succeed. I want to share classroom-tested strategies that keep every learner appropriately challenged and supported, every day. I want to explain how you and all your colleagues can conquer the fundamental challenge of teaching, then leave school each afternoon with your heads held high.

To do this I will share my own journey to the Modern Classroom model, using my story to explain the model itself. I'm not the first teacher to implement practices like these, and as you'll discover, my classroom was far from perfect.[9] But if you can understand why I started teaching this way, where I struggled and succeeded, and what I've since learned from the educators who now use these practices more effectively than I did, I'm confident that you can use this approach to meet your learners' needs too.

Here's the brief version. When I started at Eastern, my lessons didn't engage my students, and I felt like a failure. So the first step for me was to design individual lessons that could simultaneously challenge David, support Anna, and help Troy catch up. That will be your first step too, and in Part 1 (Redesigning Lessons), I'll explain how you can create better lessons.

Once my lessons were working, I encountered another challenge. David often finished early, Anna often needed more time, and Troy often missed out altogether. So what I really needed—and eventually figured out how to create—were self-paced courses, which kept David, Anna, and Troy appropriately challenged and supported for several lessons at a time. You'll encounter this challenge too, so in Part 2 (Redesigning Courses), I'll explain how you can create self-paced courses of your own.

---

[9] I often meet teachers who tell me that they used a similar approach long before they heard about MCP, or even before MCP existed. This is great! The fact that others have arrived at similar practices independently suggests to me that what I call the Modern Classroom model actually reflects general best practices for teaching and learning. And my goal in writing this book is not to claim credit for these ideas and practices, but rather to share them in a way that makes them easy for you to adapt and implement. If the techniques I describe in this book sound like things you're already doing, then I'm proud to be in good company.

Finally, once I had my own classroom running the way I wanted, I shared what I'd learned with others. My MCP co-founder Kareem Farah was the first: he visited my classroom, liked what he saw, and launched his own Modern Classroom the very next day. From there we shared our approach with our colleagues at Eastern, then with teachers across our district, then—once word got out—with thousands of educators worldwide. I want you to inspire your community too, so in Part 3 (Redesigning Instruction), I'll discuss how you can share what you've learned.

And while this book follows my path, the practices I'll share are not just my own. Far from it! I've learned a great deal from the many educators whom I've seen adapt the Modern Classroom model themselves, and I'm eager to share those insights with you too. So I've compiled here what worked for me, and what I've seen work even better for others, in hopes that you—like thousands of educators before you—can take this approach and make it your own. In each chapter that follows, I will:

- ◆ Explain a challenge that teachers face.
- ◆ Describe how I addressed that challenge in my own Modern Classroom.
- ◆ Share best practices you can use with your students, plus tips from teachers who implement these practices every day.
- ◆ Provide actionable next steps you can take right away.

After each chapter, you'll feel more confident about your ability to create a classroom in which each of your students can succeed. And by the end of the book, you'll be ready to do it.

TEACHER TIP

MARCI RICKORDS, HIGH SCHOOL ELA TEACHER (GOOSE LAKE, IOWA)

"I won't return to traditional instruction. The Modern Classroom instructional model has so many benefits for me as a teacher and for my students. Self-paced learning, differentiation, data-driven grouping, collaboration, synchronous and asynchronous learning, high-quality instructional choices—the Modern Classroom model has it all. My students' learning has become more personalized, they are more engaged, and their mastery has increased. Meanwhile I have the freedom to engage with students, I know where each student is on their path to mastery, and I'm a better teacher.

"And while this approach is initially labor-intensive, it's not reinventing the wheel. It's about taking the content you already have in place and delivering it in a research-based instructional model that meets the learning needs of all students.

"So take the plunge! Just because something appears daunting doesn't mean it can't be mastered. (This is the same advice I give students.) It will be worth it."

Your Modern Classroom Starts Here

I will warn you now that this work isn't easy. The fundamental challenge of teaching is a big one, and redesigning instruction takes time and commitment.

Yet I, like every educator, am an optimist. I know how talented our young people are, and how deeply their teachers, administrators, and families want them to succeed. I know that classrooms which meet all of their needs—which make teachers more effective, students more capable, and administrators and families more involved—exist. I've stood in them! And I know that if you follow the simple steps in this book, then you can build this kind of classroom too.

Redesigning instruction to reach students like David, Anna, and Troy isn't just possible. It's necessary! And Modern Classrooms won't just help marginalized kids at Eastern or privileged ones in Switzerland. They'll empower my kids and your kids and everyone else's kids too.

It's time to meet every learner's needs.

Part 1

Redesigning Lessons

I never set out to redesign instruction. I didn't intend to start a nonprofit, much less a movement. If you had told me when I started at Eastern that I would write a book on teaching, I would have laughed at you. I had nothing worth writing about.

What I did have were two big problems. My students weren't learning, and I was miserable.

I wasn't sure of the solutions. But what I spent most of each day actually doing was teaching lessons. If I could teach a good lesson, I figured, my students could learn—and I could feel successful.

So that was my first goal: teach a lesson that would engage David, Anna, Troy, and everyone in between.

If I could do that, I could build from there.

The Challenge of Lessons

In a traditional classroom, a teacher delivers a single lesson to all of their students at once. Those students are then expected to learn the same things in the same amount of time.

There's a problem here, and it's a big one. In fact, it's the fundamental challenge of teaching: different learners need different things.[1] So at some point in any lesson, no matter what or whom you're teaching, it's inevitable that some students will understand and be ready to move on, while other students won't. David will be bored; Anna will be lost; Troy won't be there at all. A traditional lesson will always fail to meet some learners' needs.

Of course, there are things you can do to differentiate. You can give your advanced students more challenging assignments, offer office hours for students with learning gaps, and print make-up packets for students who miss class. But these strategies just widen the gaps between learners, while creating extra work for you. They aren't sustainable for anyone.

So I believe—and have seen in Modern Classrooms worldwide—that meeting every learner's needs requires a fundamentally different approach to instruction.

For that approach to make sense, however, you must understand exactly why traditional lessons fail to offer all students the challenge and support they need. You must recognize how students like David, Anna, and Troy experience lessons like these, as well as the trade-offs their varying needs force teachers to make. Finally, you must consider what a better lesson might actually entail.

---

[1] In 2020, MCP commissioned a comprehensive literature review from the Center for Research and Reform in Education at Johns Hopkins University. That literature review begins by stating that "Research has long demonstrated that students learn at different paces and, for any age group, the variations in rates of learning are considerable…. In recent years, research on the neurology of learning has reinforced these findings." For more, see Reilly, J.M. (2020). The Modern Classrooms Project: A Review of Research-Based Best Practices. Baltimore, MD: Johns Hopkins University.

CHAPTER OBJECTIVES

By the end of this chapter, you will be able to:

1. Articulate the challenges posed by "teaching to the middle."

2. Empathize with the experiences of students whose needs traditional lessons don't meet.

3. Define the characteristics of a lesson that meets every learner's needs.

If we want all students to succeed, we need lessons that challenge, support, and engage every single learner. Here's why traditional lessons fall short.

My Problem

This isn't a book about math, and the dynamic I'll describe applies to any content area, at any grade level. But I think an example from my own experience will make the fundamental challenge of teaching concrete.

Every year in my precalculus class, I began my unit on composite functions with a problem like this:

$$\text{If } f(x) = 3x \text{ and } g(x) = x^3 + 1, \text{ evaluate } f(g(2)).$$

Functions are a core topic of high-school math, and if you understand how they work, this problem is a fun little puzzle. So David, who was proficient in algebra, solved it quickly. He raised his hand and asked for the next example.

If you don't understand what functions are, however—or if you're not sure what terms like $f(x)$ and x^3 represent in the first place—then this problem makes no sense. So Anna, who was years behind in math, didn't understand what to do. She put her head on her desk.

David needed a challenge; Anna needed support. And I knew that when Troy arrived—whether that was midway through class or the middle of next week—he would need me to explain this problem all over again.

Standing in front of the class, I felt myself growing frustrated. Why couldn't David just be patient? Why couldn't Anna just pay attention? And why couldn't Troy just show up for class? It was the first day of the unit and already I had lost my cool.

When class ended, however, I felt ashamed. David was right to advocate for himself: he was bored! It made sense why Anna would disengage from content she wasn't prepared to understand—I would have disengaged too! And I don't know why Troy was absent that day. But these young people weren't the problem. The problem was my lesson. It wasn't helping my students succeed.

So I suppose my frustration was understandable too. David, Anna, and Troy—not to mention the other twenty-plus young people in my class—simply needed different things. There was only one of me, and class was only forty-five minutes long.

What could I do?

Teaching to the Middle

When I taught a single lesson every day, I saw no way to challenge David without losing Anna, nor any way to support Anna without losing David. So I decided to aim at something in between: a lesson that would keep David interested, without leaving Anna (or, if he attended, Troy) too far behind. In other words, I "taught to the middle."

With enough effort, I could kind of make this approach work. When I gave Anna step-by-step guidance, she could make progress on complex tasks, even if David could perform them faster and without the same scaffolds. When I found "low-floor, high-ceiling" activities—tasks that Anna could tackle in a basic way and David could solve with sophistication—I could keep both students reasonably engaged. And sometimes, when I couldn't figure out how to engage both learners with the same problem, I just asked David to teach Anna.

So David stopped asking for more, Anna took her head off her desk, and Troy wasn't completely lost when he walked in. If you had come to observe my class, it might have looked like these students were really learning.

But I knew better. My lessons rarely pushed David to extend himself, while Anna came to rely on my extensive guidance. No matter how interesting my activities were, Anna always dragged along the floor, while David bumped repeatedly against the ceiling. In fact, giving David the hard questions and Anna the easy ones just widened the gaps between them. And while asking David to tutor Anna kept both students busy, it wasn't particularly fair: David deserved the chance to learn new things, while Anna needed remediation first.

Teaching this way also created a lot of extra work—I effectively had to design multiple versions of each lesson—and made it difficult for me to set consistent expectations. My class kept David and Anna engaged, but it didn't push either toward their full potential.

And to be honest, I had no idea what to do about Troy. It was hard for me to plan activities for him—I didn't know whether he'd be in class or not—and even harder for me to adjust my lesson when he did happen to arrive. I wanted him to come to class, but I dreaded the moment he walked in. I hate to say this, but my class ran more smoothly when he wasn't there.

So this was my life as a teacher, at least in my first weeks at Eastern. I stood at the board before David, Anna, Troy, and twenty of their classmates, with no way to meet all of their needs. Is it any wonder that I wanted to quit?

How Lessons Feel

If you're a teacher, this may sound familiar. If your classes were anything like mine, in fact, it might be your daily reality. Every student has different needs, and no lesson delivered to all of your students at the same time can possibly meet them all.

This isn't just in math, by the way! It's true whether you're teaching composite functions, studying a novel, conducting an experiment, learning new vocabulary, analyzing the causes of the Civil War, or doing anything else. Whenever multiple students are expected to advance through the same content at the same time:

◆ **Students like David, who are proficient or advanced, will stagnate.** These students have grade-level skills and are ready for grade-level content. Unfortunately, their classmates are not. And if you take time to help their classmates catch up, then students like David will grow bored.

   Students like David deserve to be challenged: they won't achieve their full potential if they aren't. But in lessons taught to the middle, there's just not enough to learn. So they sit in class, look for ways to entertain themselves—my highest-performing students were often my most disruptive—and fail to achieve their potential.

◆ **Students like Anna, who are far behind, will give up.** Highly scaffolded lessons help learners like Anna get by, especially in the short term. But the significant gaps in their learning make it difficult to truly understand grade-level material, or to solve challenging problems without extensive guidance from their teachers.

As a result, students like Anna lack confidence. They may advance from grade to grade, clinging to scaffolds for long enough to pass. But as her standardized-test scores revealed, Anna didn't actually understand eighth-grade math, or algebra, or geometry—and I don't think she expected to understand precalculus either. So Anna said she "wasn't good at math." Sadly, she believed it too.

And while this dynamic may feel particularly acute in math, where one skill often leads directly into the next, it exists equally in other subjects too. A student who can't write a topic sentence, for instance, will struggle to write a good paragraph—let alone an essay. A student who doesn't know why the American colonies declared independence will struggle to understand the U.S. Constitution; a student who can't conjugate verbs in the present tense will struggle to express ideas in the past or future too. Perhaps most importantly, a student who can't read at grade level will struggle in any class they ever take. Complex skills always build on foundational ones, and students with gaps in their foundations inevitably miss out.

Students like Anna want to learn. They come to class; they sit and listen. Yet they aren't prepared—we haven't adequately prepared them—to succeed. They might ask questions, if they understand enough to ask, but they also might not: they might feel embarrassed, or further inadequate if they don't understand the response. After a while, they'll stop seeing school as a place where they can succeed. So it isn't, and they don't.

◆ **Students like Troy, who are chronically absent, will fall further and further behind.** I imagine that returning to class after an absence is deeply stressful for students like Troy. They don't know what they've missed or how they'll be received when they arrive. (For teachers who must help chronically absent students catch up, these students' arrivals are stressful too.) Students like Troy must realize, however, that from the moment they enter class, they'll already be behind.

To his credit, Troy always returned. He wanted to learn and asked good questions. And I wanted to respond! But that often meant repeating myself, and losing David and Anna in the process. And if I told Troy I would answer him after class, he would spend the rest of class feeling confused. No matter what I did here, I was bound to lose someone's interest.

In theory, chronically absent students can catch up by getting notes from friends or staying after school for review. But the factors that keep students from attending school in the first place—health issues, long commutes, work or caretaking responsibilities, etc.—can make this challenging as well. And when teachers spend class delivering traditional instruction, they rarely have much time to spare. So the students who need the most support often receive the least.

Like all young people, David, Anna, and Troy want to succeed. They do their best to stay engaged, and learn what they can. But if the lessons they encounter fail to challenge them, support them, or make it easy for them to catch up, they will fail to achieve their potential.

Tragically, most traditional lessons—and therefore far too many students—fall short.

Toward Better Lessons

Ultimately I believe it is impossible for any single lesson, when delivered to a diverse group of learners at the same time, to fully meet each of those learners' needs. And this is what makes school so difficult, for teachers and students alike. The traditional lesson structure just doesn't work.

What would a better lesson look like? A better lesson would provide students like David, Anna, and Troy with an appropriate level of challenge—and allow their teacher to provide each learner with the support each actually needs. In a better lesson:

◆ **David could advance quickly through things he already knows, then spend his time learning things he doesn't.** There's little value to David in sitting through lessons on content he already understands. He'll be most engaged—and learn the most—if he can get straight to lessons that extend his understanding.

◆ **Anna could take the time she needs to understand.** Pushing Anna through content she isn't prepared to understand accomplishes very little. In fact, it's counterproductive: because she never really gets what's being taught, she develops learning gaps and begins to doubt her ability to learn in the first place.

What Anna needs is more time, so she can truly understand each new piece of content—even if that requires her to go back and patch up prerequisite skills first. Not only will this help her engage, but it will help her build self-confidence too.

◆ **Troy could start at the beginning.** It doesn't make sense for Troy to start learning midway through a lesson if he's late, or on Lesson 3 if he was absent for Lessons 1 and 2. Knowledge in every subject builds on itself, so asking Troy to learn whatever his teacher happens to be teaching when he arrives is certain to create gaps in what he understands. Instead, Troy should have the chance to start each lesson where it begins—then build up from there.

Each of these students wants to learn as much as they can, but each needs something different. A better lesson would meet each of those needs.

MASTERY CHECK

Before advancing to the next chapter, please make sure you understand how to:

☐ Articulate the challenges posed by "teaching to the middle."

☐ Empathize with the experiences of students whose needs traditional lessons don't meet.

☐ Define the characteristics of a lesson that meets every learner's needs.

Lessons like the ones I've just described may sound impossible to create. They aren't. They begin with a new form of instruction.

Digitize Direct Instruction

Every lesson involves some transfer of knowledge. You know things that your learners don't, and you want your learners to know those things too. So you teach.

There are many ways you could transfer this knowledge. You could tell your students to read a book or have them conduct an experiment or take them on a field trip. At some point, however, you'll probably just want to explain something to them. In other words, you'll want to provide direct instruction.

The fact that every learner is different makes direct instruction difficult. If David and Anna are sitting in front of you, it's impossible to explain composite functions without either boring David or losing Anna. And if Troy is absent, he's going to miss out altogether. If you explain something new to your whole class at once, therefore, you won't meet every learner's needs.

What *you* need is a better way to deliver direct instruction.

CHAPTER OBJECTIVES

By the end of this chapter, you will be able to:

1. Create instructional videos that students can access anytime, anywhere, and at their own paces.

2. Engage students in learning actively from instructional videos.

3. Explain the role that technology plays in Modern Classrooms.

As you read my story and discover practices that work for Modern Classroom educators worldwide, consider this: how can you explain what you know in a way that helps every student— whether they are ahead, behind, or absent—achieve their full potential?

My Story: One Small Step

By October of my first year at Eastern, I was ready to quit. But at the beginning of November, I attended a day of professional development. That afternoon, in a presentation by a math teacher named Nick Bennett, my life changed forever.

Nick taught precalculus at another school in my district. In his presentation, he explained the simple process he used to deliver direct instruction. It involved three steps:

1. He mounted a video camera above his desk and recorded himself solving a math problem.

2. He posted that video online, then used a platform called Edpuzzle to insert questions at key points in the video.

3. He shared his videos with his students, who could watch—and answer the Edpuzzle questions—at their own paces, at home or in school.

Then Nick spent class time answering students' questions and reviewing their work.

Nick's process was simple, but its implications were profound. I realized that, if I replaced my live explanations with videos:

◆ **I could make instruction more accessible.** Instead of explaining new concepts to the students who happened to be in my classroom at any given time, I could use videos to explain the same concepts to all of my students—whether they were in class or not. Students could fast-forward if they already understood, or pause and re-watch if something didn't make sense. They could watch outside of class too, and share my videos with their families if they needed additional help.

◆ **I could be clearer and more concise.** When I tried to deliver direct instruction live, I always spent a lot of time and energy trying to hold my students' attention. Not only was this exhausting, but it also meant that direct instruction often dragged on: every time I had to redirect behavior or answer a question, I paused my explanation. On video, however, I could deliver the same explanation without interruption. A five-minute video could explain a concept that might otherwise take twenty minutes to present live, and I could answer questions one-on-one as they arose.

◆ **I could ask better questions and collect better data.** Instead of asking questions live and calling on a few students to answer, I could use the questions embedded in my videos to ask every student every question I wanted to pose. Answering questions online would be more comfortable for my students, who could respond without fear of being wrong in front of their peers. And every time I added a question, I could analyze student responses to see exactly what each of my students did and did not yet understand.

◆ **I could work more closely with students during class.** Instead of lecturing from my whiteboard, I could spend class walking around my room, answering questions and providing encouragement. My students could ask me questions without feeling embarrassed, and I could take the time to answer—and to build relationships—without interrupting other students' learning.

◆ **I could foster greater collaboration.** Rather than spending my time and energy keeping students quiet while I lectured, I could ask students to watch my videos independently, then encourage them to work together to apply what they had learned. Because my videos were shorter than my live explanations, students would have more time to collaborate. This would help them learn—and make life easier for me too.

Videos with embedded questions, I realized, would also improve my students' learning experiences. With a video on composite functions, for instance:

◆ **David would no longer feel held back.** He could move quickly through the video explanation, demonstrating his understanding as he went. Once he finished, he could get straight to work on more challenging problems.

◆ **Anna would no longer feel rushed.** She could pause the video at points where she was confused, and rewatch particular segments if necessary. She could also ask me or her classmates questions without disrupting the rest of the class, and watch again after school if necessary.

◆ **Troy would no longer feel lost.** Whenever he arrived, he could start my video from the beginning. He could watch quickly if he understood, or rewatch or ask questions if he didn't. If he was able, he could also use my videos to catch up at home.[1]

I had never recorded an instructional video before, and I didn't know how my students would respond. Yet I knew my traditional approach wasn't working. I felt that videos might. And while I knew there were plenty of math videos online, I was inspired by Nick and wanted to try recording my own.

So I went home that evening, started a video call with myself, hit the record button, and explained how to evaluate composite functions. Then I created an account on Edpuzzle, uploaded my recording, and inserted questions at key points in the video. When I got to school the next morning, I borrowed one of Eastern's laptop carts, posted the link to my video on my learning management system, and waited eagerly for my students to arrive.

I was nervous about trying something new, but excited to see if it would work. And for the first time in weeks, I didn't find myself dreading the first-period bell.

My first day of video instruction was far from perfect. Some of my students struggled to find the video, and others seemed confused about its purpose. But most seemed pleasantly surprised: they didn't like traditional lessons any more than I did. And I'll never forget the delight on my students' faces when they realized that the voice coming from their screens was actually mine. "Wait, Mr. Barnett," several exclaimed, "this is *you* in the video?!" I beamed. Then I walked around the room, answering questions and providing encouragement while every student learned.

That day, I saw and felt things as a teacher that I'd never experienced before. I saw David's face light up: he sped through the video, then moved directly into challenging practice problems.

---

[1] I didn't actually know if Troy would be able to catch up at home, so I didn't require it. Some learners have better access to support outside of class—technology, tutoring, etc.—than do others, so it isn't fair to expect that all students can learn equally at home. But it is fair to give all students that opportunity. And it creates, for all students, the possibility that others in their lives—parents, guardians, coaches, siblings, mentors, etc.—can watch these videos too, and therefore participate more actively in those students' learning.

I saw Anna breathe a sigh of relief: she paused the video several times to ask me questions, then found friends to work with on post-video practice. And when Troy arrived midway through class, I saw him grab a laptop and get straight to work.

Watching my students learn from my video and then from each other, I felt a new and unfamiliar sense of calm. My students' learning no longer depended on my tenuous ability to control their behavior while delivering an engaging presentation from the front of my room. Instead, each student could learn from me—through my video—at their own pace, and I was always there to support. It was beautiful. And I knew in that moment that I'd never go back to traditional teaching again.

Creating my first video was just the start of my Modern Classroom journey: as I'll explain throughout this book, I spent the rest of that year at Eastern designing a classroom that unlocked videos' full pedagogical potential, and I've now spent a decade refining that approach even further. There's much more to Modern Classrooms than videos, and I'm eager to share it all.

But replacing my live explanation with that video was a critical first step. It should be yours too—as it has been for thousands of other educators. And while it's one small step for you to take now, it will be a giant leap for your career.

If you're ready to make your instruction more accessible, free up class time to work closely with your students, and start meeting every learner's needs in the process, here's what you can do.

Practice 1.1: Provide Clear, Focused Explanations

There are many ways to make direct instruction more accessible. You can record your own videos, or you can use videos you find online. You can share podcasts, websites, or any other resource that helps your students learn.[2] What matters is that your students can access the content they need whenever they are ready to learn it, and that they can take the time they need to learn it fully.

---

[2] These resources don't even need to be digital: the once-revolutionary technology we now call "books" can also help students learn asynchronously. That's what they used in one-room schoolhouses! But we live in a digital world, and I've found that digital resources are often most engaging for students.

Whatever form(s) of direct instruction you provide, aim for explanations that:

◆ **Have one clear learning objective.** Each digital resource you provide should help students learn a single new skill or concept. This helps both you and your students stay focused. It's better to create multiple discrete explanations than to cover multiple objectives simultaneously.

◆ **Are as concise as possible.** Keeping digital direct instruction concise respects students' attention spans, limits time spent on screens, and frees up time for students to work together face to face. Students should learn what they need to know as efficiently as possible, then close their devices and engage in more collaborative learning activities.

◆ **Keep things simple.** Cognitive load theory suggests that, because students have a finite amount of working memory, the most effective instruction maximizes students' ability to learn by minimizing extraneous demands on their attention. If you want learners to focus on the substance of what you're explaining, in other words, don't get fancy with style. Think large and legible text, ample spacing, and contrasting colors. This also makes learning more accessible to students with visual impairments.

◆ **Use visuals purposefully.** A clear and relevant image can support your explanation, but an unclear or irrelevant one can divert learners' precious attention. Ultimately, digital direct instruction doesn't need to look pretty: it needs to help learners understand. Look for visual elements that enhance understanding and avoid any that don't.

◆ **Include opportunities for engagement.** Learning should be an active experience: rather than simply sitting and consuming content, you want students engaging with instruction while it's delivered. Think ahead about the points in your explanations when students can participate, then give them something to do at each of those points. Digital direct instruction allows for greater learner engagement than does traditional teaching—in a video with embedded questions, every learner can answer every question—but this requires planning ahead.

None of these recommendations should be particularly surprising: they are the characteristics of an effective live presentation too! A good explanation is a good explanation, no matter how it's delivered. A good digital explanation, however, makes learning accessible anytime, anywhere—and empowers you to work closely with individual learners during class. No live lesson can do that.

TEACHER TIP

WHITNEI MOORE, MIDDLE SCHOOL SPECIAL EDUCATION TEACHER (CHICAGO, ILLINOIS)

"I try very hard to keep my videos around seven to ten minutes. I have had the most student success and engagement when I keep my videos relatively short. My students love being able to 'pause me' and jot down notes while watching videos. During my live in-person lessons, my students often say that I talk too fast (I'm a stickler for staying on schedule), so this gives them the opportunity to slow down the lesson to the pace that works best for their learning style."

Practice 1.2: Make Instruction Feel Personal

In my opinion, the best way to digitize direct instruction is to create your own instructional videos. This isn't necessary—you can experience the many benefits of digital direct instruction by using other videos as well—but I've found it's more engaging for students and more satisfying for teachers too. I recorded videos myself, and thousands of Modern Classroom educators record their own videos every day.

This can take a lot of work, especially at first. You'll need to find a recording process that works; you'll make mistakes and need to troubleshoot; you'll finish a video and realize that you want to do the whole thing again. Recording a good video often takes longer than either explaining something live or finding a decent video of someone else explaining it.

Yet I still recommend you take the time to create videos yourself. In my experience, recording your own videos:

◆ **Helps you be clear.** To create a short, focused video, you really need to understand why your content matters—and how you can explain it most simply. Planning a video forces you to explain things in a clear, concise way. That's always worthwhile.

◆ **Lets you tailor instruction to your own students' needs.** You know your learners better than anyone else. You know where they come from, what they care about, and what kind of explanations will make most sense to them. If you record your own videos, you can explain your content in ways you know they'll understand.

◆ **Demonstrates your expertise.** You don't need someone else to explain things you already know! Your students should recognize that you are an expert in your content, and therefore that they can trust you to answer their questions. Creating videos shows them that.

◆ **Helps learners (and their families) get to know you.** Once you get comfortable, recording videos becomes fun. You can let your personality shine through, while sharing things about yourself that your learners might like to know. If your learners watch these videos at home, it's a great way for their families to meet you too.

When you record your own videos, you effectively clone yourself: your students can learn from you anytime, anywhere, then rewatch your explanations as many times as they need. When they're in class with you, they have an expert just a few steps away. And once you've recorded a good video, you can use it for the rest of your teaching career! Creating that video is an up-front investment of time that will make your life easier for many years to come.

Recording your first video, however, can feel daunting. It certainly felt that way to me! When I started, I didn't know what technology to use, or how to use it, and I was scared to make mistakes on videos that might exist online forever.

Yet over time I developed a method that worked for me, and this process became easy to replicate. I found programs I was comfortable using, and accepted that mistakes are a natural part of teaching and learning. (I certainly made plenty while lecturing from my whiteboard.) Correcting my mistakes in real time helped me model to my students the growth mindsets I wanted them to develop.

And I knew my students would appreciate my videos, flaws and all, so I just decided to go for it! I even started having some fun.

The simple recording method I used was as follows:

1. Start an online video call with myself, using a platform like Zoom, Google Meet, or Microsoft Teams.

2. Hit the record button.

3. Explain, using slides I'd created in advance, something new.

4. Stop recording.

5. Save the video.

6. Share it with my students.

This method wasn't fancy, and it evolved as I experimented with different programs and techniques. But my students appreciated the simplicity of my videos, as well as the effort I'd made to record them. If you're willing to try, I think they'll appreciate your videos too.

If you do decide to record your own videos, I recommend that you:

◆ **Use the technology you have.** You don't need anything special to create a good video—just a computer and a way of recording your screen. If you can join a video call, you can record a video! Just start a call with yourself and hit Record.

   If your school provides you with dedicated video-recording software, you can use that too. (I actually recommend it, because you can ask your colleagues for help.) Most recording programs have helpful and easy-to-follow guidance online.[3]

◆ **Minimize text on-screen.** The easiest way to present content in a video is with a slideshow that you speak over—just like you might use if presenting live. While creating your

---

[3] I want this book to stand the test of time, so I won't go too deeply into specific recording platforms (which can always change) here. For up-to-date guidance on the tools I recommend, like (as of September 2024) Edpuzzle, Screencastify, and ScreenPal, visit www.meeteverylearnersneeds.org. Ultimately, the program you choose doesn't really matter—they all do similar things anyway—so my main recommendation is to find something you can figure out how to use, then go with it.

slideshows, remember that it can be hard to read something and listen at the same time. So if you want your students to listen to what you say, you should present only essential text—and make it big and easy to read.[4]

◆ **Use animations and/or annotations.** If you use slides to present text and/or images, adding animations that display new elements sequentially helps keep learners focused. And if you're annotating text or solving a problem, on-screen drawing tools can help you write on your screen in the same way you'd write on a whiteboard. These enhancements aren't necessary, but they are nice.

◆ **Be natural.** Imagine you're an online tutor, explaining something new. Speak in a conversational way, and don't worry about speaking too fast: your students are less likely to get bored, and they can always pause and rewatch if they miss something. Your videos should be relatable and engaging—just like you would explain things in person!

If possible, it's also nice to include your face somewhere in the video: this adds a personal touch and ensures that there's always something dynamic happening on the screen. If you have a webcam, most recording platforms make this easy. If not, that's okay too.

◆ **Accept imperfection.** It's impossible to create a perfect video, so don't try! I recommend you adopt an informal one-take rule: do a quick practice run, then record your entire video in one go. If you catch a mistake while recording, you can address it in real time; if you realize it afterward, you can use a tool like Edpuzzle to insert a text comment correcting it. And if you really feel the need to re-record, you can. But remember that mistakes are inevitable, and that you make them while lecturing too. The flaws in your videos are often what makes them—and you—relatable.

---

[4] For students who like reading, or students who have difficulty with audio or visual processing, adding captions can make your videos more accessible. Most screen-recording programs can generate good captions automatically, and you can use a variety of programs to translate these captions into different languages too. You can find more guidance on adding captions at www.meeteverylearnersneeds.org.

◆ **Just do it.** Ultimately, the only way to create a video is to sit down and record one! And you won't know how powerful your own videos can be until you give recording a try.

So set aside some time, record your screen, and explain something new! You'll encounter challenges along the way, but that's part of the learning process. Recording gets *much* easier over time. You'll develop a new skill in the meantime, and I bet you'll even have some fun.

And if I haven't convinced you to try recording, that's okay too! You should use whatever resources you think are best for you and your students. There are plenty of good videos already out there, many of which follow the research-based best practices I've described.[5] If you can find existing videos that engage your students, both you and they can still enjoy the benefits of digital direct instruction.

In fact, while I recorded my own videos for each precalculus lesson I taught, I often used other videos to supplement my instruction. When students needed to review foundational skills, for instance, I sent them to videos I had found online: this saved me from having to create videos on many years' worth of prerequisite content. And when I taught in Switzerland, where many of my students were not native English speakers, I encouraged students to seek out explanations in their native languages where helpful.[6] Using other videos in these ways added variety, and helped me further support struggling students, without creating too much extra work.

Finally, if you aren't sure what videos to use or how to make your own videos engaging, ask your students! Mine told me that they preferred learning from me, even if my videos weren't fancy. So I kept on recording.

---

[5] For recommended sources of engaging instructional videos—as well as MCP-created videos aligned to several common curricula—please visit www.meetevery learnersneeds.org.

[6] My class still required students to develop their English skills: my whole-class and small-group activities were in English, as were my Mastery Checks and other assessments. But I found that allowing—and at times encouraging—my students to consume content in their native languages helped them grow both as mathematicians and as English speakers. Seeing content first in the languages they spoke fluently often helped them participate more actively in activities conducted in English.

JACKIE DURR, MIDDLE SCHOOL ELA TEACHER (RESTON, VIRGINIA)

"My videos aren't Hollywood productions, but they are predictable; my students are used to my pace, cadence, bad jokes, and children's cameos. I use basic animations and annotations, nothing super flashy. My video philosophy is that if I were doing it live, it would never be perfect, so I don't add that pressure to myself when making videos either!

"For me, the magic length of a video is six to eight minutes."

Practice 1.3: Plan for Active Engagement

Videos make direct instruction accessible. But if your students just sit and watch those videos passively, they may not learn much. You wouldn't just stand at the board, ask students to sit quietly, and expect them to learn, would you?

Good instruction requires students to participate. So just as you might involve learners in traditional direct instruction, you should engage your students in your digital explanations too. I recommend that you:

◆ **Insert questions and/or text comments.** Before I used videos, I struggled to track what each of my students actually understood. When I asked questions in class, the same few students would always want to answer. Calling on students at random was stressful. And there was a natural limit to how many students I could ask.

With videos, however, you can use a platform like Edpuzzle to insert questions at key points throughout your explanation, then require each learner to answer every question. (You can add questions to your own videos or to other videos you find online.) This removes the stress of live questioning and gives you comprehensive data about your students' understanding. If you can display the correct response after every question—and explain why other responses are incorrect—you can give every learner immediate feedback too.

Most platforms that let you embed questions also let you insert text comments, which pause the video for students to read. Adding a text comment is a great way to correct mistakes you may have made during your explanation, or to add in points you may have forgotten to make. Knowing that you can go back and add comments should make recording videos less stressful in the first place.

The programs available to insert questions and/or text comments in videos evolve all the time, so I won't give detailed instructions on how to use them here.[7] Whatever platform you use, however, remember that adding a few timely questions—the same questions you would ask while explaining this content live to your students, in the same places—can make watching videos an active and highly engaging way to learn. And once you can insert text comments, you never have to worry about making mistakes again.

◆ **Support student note-taking.** Taking guided notes helps students stay engaged while watching videos, and reviewing those notes helps students retain what they have learned. The act of writing something down helps transfer it to memory, and notes are invaluable resources when unit- or year-end assessments come around.

If you create slides for your videos, one easy way to encourage note-taking is simply to print out copies of your video slides—with key information removed—then ask your students to fill in that information as they watch. This doesn't require much extra planning, but it gives learners something valuable to do during the video.

If you'd like to give students more autonomy, there are other note-taking strategies you can use: I often used the Cornell note-taking system, and I've seen teachers use a variety of graphic organizers to help students retain video content.[8] Or, if you prefer, you can simply ask your students to take notes on blank paper.

---

[7] As with video-recording software, I recommend you visit www.meeteverylearner sneeds.org for up-to-date guidance on programs for video engagement. There you'll also see examples of videos with embedded questions and text comments.

[8] Visit www.meeteverylearnersneeds.org to see, download, and customize a variety of different note-taking templates. And don't worry—the resources there are free!

Whatever note-taking strategy you use, I recommend that you:

◆ **Teach note-taking explicitly.** Don't assume that your students know how to take good notes—or that they'll figure this out on their own. To help your students get started, you can create a video that models good note-taking, or prepare a few sets of exemplary notes. Be explicit about the purpose of note-taking, as well as the characteristics of effective notes.

◆ **Review learners' notes and provide feedback.** If you want your students to take note-taking seriously, make a point of reviewing the notes that students do take, especially early in the year. Tell each of your students what they are doing well, and how their notes can be improved. This takes time, but it's worth it: the sooner you can get every learner taking good notes, the more each will learn.

◆ **Help learners keep their notes organized.** Good notes are a valuable resource, so you don't want students to lose them. If your students struggle to keep their papers organized (as mine often did), consider instituting a binder or folder system that keeps students' notes secure and well-organized. It's not the end of the world if students do lose their notes—the exercise of note-taking is valuable in itself, and students can always go back and retake notes from your videos. But it's nice to teach students good organizational habits, too.

Finally, I strongly recommend that students take notes on paper. While I understand the appeal of digital notes—nothing to print or lose—there's something valuable about teaching students to take notes by hand. It builds a skill that learners can use in many contexts, and it reduces the cognitive load on students: rather than toggling back and forth between a video and digital notes, they can watch your instruction on their screens while taking notes on paper.

Both embedded questions and note-taking routines make digital direct instruction an active and rewarding experience for learners, whether they watch in class or at home. And these retention strategies can work nicely together too: if you use embedded questions and guided notes, you can pause your videos to remind students to take notes! That's a great way to keep every learner engaged—and help them retain what you want them to know.

TEACHER TIP

LAURA SUCKERMAN, FOURTH GRADE TEACHER (ROBBINSDALE, MINNESOTA)

"Creating videos has been life-changing: I feel like I have cloned myself. Students are able to watch the videos at their own pace and rewatch as needed, while parents can watch with their students and send a consistent message and process for solving problems or learning skills. I am now able to ensure that all students are getting the same instruction, and that they can work at their own pace. This allows the students that excel at certain topics or subjects to work ahead to learning that challenges them, and gives the students that struggle or need more time the flexibility they need.

"To support every student's learning, I give them guided notes with questions to complete before, during, and after the instructional video. I begin the year with specific prompts for students to complete, then transition to a more open style of note-taking as the year progresses and as students become ready for them. This is a key way for me to differentiate for different learners, as some will be ready for open notes earlier than others and some will always need the guiding questions."

Practice 1.4: Get Your Devices Ready

Video instruction only works if your students have a way to watch. And while some students may be able to watch at home, some may not—so you'll need a way for students to watch in class.[9] If students watch in class, you can also respond to questions as soon as they arise, while helping your students take good notes.

If you don't have the technology on hand to let students watch in class, you may need to get creative. At Eastern I didn't have much technology either, so I scrounged up a few old desktop computers from colleagues who rarely used them, bought cheap headphone splitters online (so multiple students could watch a

---

[9] While it's great that students in Modern Classrooms can watch videos at home, I don't think this is fair to expect. This distinguishes Modern Classrooms from "flipped classrooms," in which students are generally expected to watch videos at home and solve problems together in class. The other key distinction, which I'll explain in Part 2, is that Modern Classrooms are self-paced, so students in the same class may be working on different things at the same time.

video together), and borrowed my school's laptop carts whenever they were available. That was usually enough.

Most importantly, however, I kept my videos short and tried to get learners working off-screen as soon as possible. And once my learners started progressing at their own paces—which I'll explain soon—I found that, at any given time, only a handful of students actually needed computers: the rest were working together, or directly with me, on whiteboards or on paper. So a few desktops, which effectively formed a video-watching station, were plenty.

If tech access is a challenge for you too, then I encourage you to be similarly resourceful. Look for unused devices, find ways for students to share the devices you do have, or let students bring their own devices (if possible) to class. Where there's a will, there's a way.

And even if you have enough devices for all of your students, you should still aim to make learning from videos as quick and efficient as possible. Minimizing the time that students spend on-screen, whether by necessity or by choice, fosters collaboration and connection. Whatever technology you and your students use, make sure you use it purposefully—and get students learning off-screen as soon as they are ready.[10]

TEACHER TIP

GABRIELA BELTRAMO, MIDDLE SCHOOL SPANISH TEACHER (SÃO PAULO, BRAZIL)

"My school provides each student with a tablet or a computer, which students can use to access my videos and assignments. Some students prefer to use their own devices instead, which is fine with me.

"At the start of the year, I show all of my students how to navigate my learning management system, step-by-step. I also give them an exercise to practice finding the right path to follow. Before long, they can do everything themselves."

---

[10] Even as technology becomes more common in our schools, most teachers receive surprisingly little training on how to use it—and the training they do receive often explains how certain programs and devices functionally work, not how they can be used pedagogically. Compared to traditional teachers at the same schools, therefore, Modern Classroom educators were significantly more likely to report that they use technology effectively. See Wolf, B., Eisinger, J., & Ross, S. (2020). The Modern Classrooms Project: Survey Results for the 2019–20 School Year. Baltimore, MD: Johns Hopkins University.

Takeaways: Technology's Limited Role

Videos are amazing instructional tools. They make learning accessible, free you up to work closely with learners during class, and—once you have them—save you countless hours of repetition. After I had recorded my first video, I couldn't believe how much more time I had to interact with my students.

But videos are just that: tools. No video can replace a caring teacher. Nor can videos alone help most learners achieve mastery. A class that's too reliant on videos can quickly become dull for students and teachers alike, or impede the social and emotional learning that comes from working closely with peers and adults. Technology should serve to enhance these human interactions, not get in the way.

So use videos, but keep them concise, engaging, and (if possible) personal. The shorter your videos are, the more time students will have to learn from one another. The more your embedded questions and guided notes hold your students' attention, the more they'll retain. And the better your videos address your students' needs and interests, the more your students will care to engage.

A good instructional video, in fact, is ultimately quite similar to a good lesson delivered live. It's focused, it's dynamic, and it includes regular checks for understanding. Unlike a traditional lesson, however, a video can also be watched (and re-watched) anytime, anywhere, and it frees you up during class.

Whether you record them yourself or not, instructional videos help you explain content more clearly, more efficiently, and more accessibly. That helps everyone in your classroom succeed.

MASTERY CHECK

Before advancing to the next chapter, please make sure you understand how to:

☐ Create instructional videos that students can access anytime, anywhere, and at their own paces.

☐ Engage students in learning actively from instructional videos.

☐ Explain the role that technology plays in Modern Classrooms.

Digitizing your direct instruction is a huge accomplishment—and a critical first step. It's what students do after accessing direct instruction, however, that makes Modern Classrooms special.

Step 2

Get Learners Working Together

Digitizing direct instruction helps students access content. But to develop real understanding—and to grow as human beings—young people must work together. Collaborating helps students tackle common challenges, build interpersonal skills, and develop understanding even without a teacher's help. In fact, the opportunity to learn with and from classmates is much of what makes going to school valuable in the first place.

In traditional lessons, the interactions between learners are often limited. During direct instruction, for instance, students are usually expected to be quiet while the teacher speaks. Traditional lesson plans also impose time limits on collaborative activities, which can make it hard for students to engage beyond a surface level—especially if these activities are shortened when live instruction, as it often does, takes longer than expected. And when some students in a class are bored, others are lost, and others aren't there at all, it's often hard for them to have meaningful discussions in the first place.

Digitizing direct instruction removes many of these constraints. You no longer need to keep students quiet while you lecture. Your students can interact before, during, and after your videos. And they have more time to work with one another, both in and out of class, because your content is available whenever and wherever students need it. Once your students take advantage of these opportunities to work productively together, their academic and social development will flourish.

All you need to do is show them how.

CHAPTER OBJECTIVES

By the end of this chapter, you will be able to:

1. Plan opportunities for learners to work together after accessing direct instruction.

2. Foster a culture of organic collaboration.

3. Set up your classroom to support group work.

This is, of course, easier said than done—especially when digital direct instruction makes it so easy for students to learn on their own. So in a classroom designed to meet each individual learner's needs, how do you get students working with, and learning from, one another?

My Story: What Comes Next?

I soon got better at creating engaging videos, and my students got accustomed to learning from them. They would come in, watch my video, answer my embedded questions, and take guided notes. Then they would ask, "What should we do next?"

This wasn't always an easy question to answer. While my students generally learned much more quickly from my videos than they had from traditional direct instruction—without the interruptions of behavior management and whole-class questioning, it's amazing how fast students can learn—they didn't all progress at the same paces. David usually finished early, Anna usually needed to re-watch or ask questions, and Troy usually started the lesson late. I needed something for each of them to do as soon as they finished the video, no matter when that was.

I also wanted a way for my students to work together. Videos made it easy for them to learn independently, but I wanted them to answer each other's questions, encourage one another, and build their social and problem-solving skills in the process. My classroom had become very calm, but I wanted to feel and hear the dynamic buzz that comes when students learn together.

So I developed a consistent routine. My students would start each class by watching a new video. After watching, they would put their computers away, find classmates who had also finished the video, and spend most of class working together on practice problems, off-screen, while I provided support. Finally, at the end of class, each student would complete a short Exit Ticket to show what they had learned.

This was a nice balance between independent and collaborative learning, and over time it became quite efficient. My videos became more concise and my students became more comfortable answering embedded questions and taking notes, so the time students spent watching videos started to decrease; as a result, students spent more and more of class interacting face to face. The real learning in my class, I realized, didn't happen when students watched my videos and listened to me. It happened when they worked together to apply the concepts I had used my videos to introduce.

I've now seen this kind of authentic, productive collaboration in Modern Classrooms in every grade level and subject area. It's a beautiful thing. And if you're ready to bring it to life in your own classroom, here's what you can do.

Practice 2.1: Prepare Video-Aligned Practice

Watching a video is a great way to learn something new, especially if students are answering embedded questions and taking good notes. But a single short video, no matter how engaging or clear, will rarely be enough to give learners a deep understanding of a new concept or skill.

After each video, therefore, students should take what they've just seen and apply it through practice. Depending on what you teach, practice activities might include readings, worksheets, small-group discussions, labs, simulations, games, or anything else that helps your learners apply what they learn in your videos.[1] And if your curriculum already contains activities that students can complete individually or in small groups, use those! Your goals here are to get students thinking and help them build understanding.

In general, effective post-video practice:

◆ **Builds on your direct instruction.** The work you give learners should feel like a natural extension of your video (or other digital direct instruction), so that learners will know exactly how to begin. It should also help students extend their understanding beyond what you can cover in a brief instructional video.

---

[1] For examples of effective practice activities from a wide range of grade levels and subject areas, visit www.meeteverylearnersneeds.org.

◆ **Happens off-screen.** Students will use devices to watch your videos, but the best practice is usually hands-on. Working on paper facilitates collaboration, and helps you see what students are (or aren't) doing. It's also easier to give students direct feedback on their work when you can see it on paper than when they are typing and submitting it online.

   With that said, there are good platforms for learning online, and it's nice when digital activities can provide students immediate feedback. So it's okay to give students on-screen practice too, especially if they can work on it together. You know your learners best, so I encourage you to find what works best for them.

◆ **Can be completed independently or in small groups.** Students should be able to complete practice activities without much direction or supervision from you: this keeps you free to provide support wherever it's needed, and also helps students like Troy catch up if they miss class. If students know exactly what each practice activity requires, they can move straight from videos into practice, and they can support one another without needing to ask you for help. So try your best to make these activities simple, and keep your directions clear.[2]

The content in your videos should feel new and challenging to your learners: that's why you share videos in the first place. But by the time students complete their practice, this content should feel familiar. That's how your students will know they understand it.

   And if you want to try a more inquiry-based approach, consider giving your students practice activities to complete *before* the video as well. That way, students can attempt unfamiliar tasks without your guidance at first, then use your video to understand the concepts they have just encountered. This gives students the chance to grow through productive struggle, and means they will be eager to watch your video explanation: the video will help them

---

[2] If your curriculum emphasizes whole-class instruction, you may need to adapt whole-class activities so that they can be completed independently or in small groups. You can see examples of student-led practice activities from several common curricula at www.meeteverylearnersneeds.org.

understand the questions they have just struggled to answer! They can then apply that newfound understanding on collaborative, post-video practice.[3]

TEACHER TIP

JOANNA SCHINDEL, HIGH SCHOOL ELL TEACHER (OVERLAND PARK, KANSAS)

"After my videos, I provide students with different ways to practice English across multiple language domains. Students engage individually, with peers, and as a whole class.

"Usually, they begin with an activity similar to what I showed in my video. Then, they can work with a partner to review flashcards, practice vocabulary, or build their language skills in other ways. Finally, we end each class with a whole-group communicative practice activity that allows all students to practice using the language in spoken conversations.

"This kind of collaboration in a language learning environment is especially important, because helping students feel a sense of belonging and connection ensures that students feel safe and comfortable taking risks. That being said, this model allows me to make adjustments on days when students are struggling to engage with other learners. I can also provide opportunities for one-on-one instruction or individualized versions of group tasks if necessary."

Practice 2.2: Make Practice Collaborative

A good video, combined with good practice, can help any learner understand anything. But it's a lot easier to learn—and to teach—if your students can work together.

Collaboration between students has several important benefits. It builds community, develops valuable soft skills, and helps learners

---

[3] This inquiry-based approach is actually my preferred method of teaching in a Modern Classroom, as I think it represents the most authentic form of learning: students try a new and unfamiliar task, then watch a video that helps them, then succeed in completing that task. The explanation you provide has obvious value to the learner, because it helps them do something they previously could not.

With that said, it's often easier to introduce collaborative post-video practice first, then build up to inquiry-based learning once students feel comfortable with both video learning and the idea of productive struggle. As with every Modern Classroom practice, I encourage you to do what feels right for you and your learners.

internalize content. It also saves you work, while offering students more immediate support: if learners can answer each other's questions, they don't have to wait for you to respond.

Valuable as it is, collaboration doesn't always come naturally to young people. They may feel intimidated by the prospect of working with classmates they don't yet know. They may feel nervous about contributing their ideas. And while they may have shared answers or copied notes before, they may never have engaged deeply in learning with their peers.

So if you want your students to feel comfortable practicing together, you may have to provide some structure for collaboration—especially at the start of the year. You can:

◆ **Suggest (or require) that students complete practice together.** One simple way to do this is to have students write the name of their partners on the practice work they complete. You can also ask students to have their peers review or "sign off" on practice work before they submit it.

◆ **Encourage students to ask each other for support.** Modern Classroom educators often request that their students ask classmates for help before asking the teacher. (One common formulation is "Ask Three Before Me.") You don't have to make this a strict rule, but it's nice to remind students who come to you with questions that they can always ask their classmates first. Most of the time, asking a classmate for help will be faster than waiting for you to provide it. And while it's most natural for students to work together during practice, they can answer each other's questions while watching videos too.

◆ **Explain to students why they should collaborate—and celebrate them when they do.** Practice activities that encourage or require collaboration provide great opportunities for students to work together. The most authentic collaboration, however, occurs naturally, when students ask each other for help—and provide it—without your prompting. And in a Modern Classroom, where students are free to choose whom they work with and when, there is ample opportunity for it.

So if you want your students to work together spontaneously, make sure they know how it benefits them. Emphasize that the more students collaborate, the easier and more productive it will become. And when you see students working together productively without your prompting, say something! This kind of positive reinforcement helps make organic collaboration a habit.

Getting students to work together isn't always easy, and your students may resist it at first. Mine certainly did! But if you create clear avenues for collaboration, and explain how working together benefits your students, they will figure it out before long. And once they do, learning will become easier—and likely more fun—for everyone involved.

TEACHER TIP

LIZ ROSENBERG, KINDERGARTEN TEACHER (WASHINGTON, DISTRICT OF COLUMBIA)

"My students who receive extra help through peer collaboration have always willingly accepted it. We spend a lot of time talking through what it means to be a helper rather than giving another kid an answer. One thing I say all the time is, 'If you tell your friend the answer, then your brain is learning, but it does not give them a chance to learn.'

"I also spend a lot of time talking about the importance of learning with other people and reminding my students that our purpose in school is to learn and to take care of each other. We talk about the fact that when you can explain your thinking to someone else, it helps you learn more. When that is explicitly stated as a norm, it's much easier to get students to participate.

"Often the students who learn quickly are academically strong but have many social skills to develop. So when they support their classmates, the growth and help goes both ways."

Practice 2.3: Designate Space for Group Work

If your students are going to work in groups, they need spaces where that is easy to do. While they'll want quiet places to watch your videos and take notes, they'll also need places where they can discuss, solve problems, and ultimately learn together.

If you can, therefore, I recommend that you dedicate spaces in your classroom for both individual and collaborative work. In your quiet-work spaces, students can watch videos, take notes, and complete assessments without being distracted. These can be tables that are designated for individual work or rows of desks facing the same direction.

For collaborative work, I recommend you use small tables or clusters of desks—three to six is ideal—where students can easily work together. If possible, it can also be nice to put these near white-boards, so that students can brainstorm or solve problems collaboratively. Figure 2.1 shows how my classroom was organized.

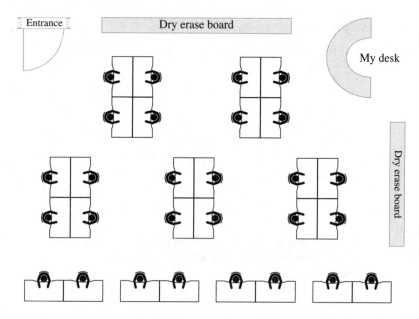

FIGURE 2.1
The layout of my classroom at Eastern. Students could work independently at the back of the room, or collaborate with their classmates at the four-desk tables in the front and middle. This is only one of many possible arrangements that can support both individual and group work.

Designating spaces in this way has several benefits. First, it establishes clear expectations for students: in individual-work spaces, they can work quietly, and when sitting with their class-mates, they can work together. Second, it helps you provide appropriate supports: you can check in briefly with students working independently, but spend most of your time facilitating discourse and collaboration between students working in groups. Finally, it can get your students up and moving during class, which is good for both their bodies and their minds.

In this way, a Modern Classroom often resembles a college library. You'll see groups of learners studying together at tables, as well as spaces for learners to work independently. Some students will be on computers, and some won't. It might look chaotic from the outside, but there's a clear logic organizing it all. Most importantly, every learner in your classroom can access the support they need.

Your exact setup will obviously depend on your own classroom space, and you don't need to be too strict here: it's fine if students watch videos at tables together, and you can always rearrange your room when necessary.[4] But the more you can design spaces where students can collaborate naturally, the more likely they'll be to work together productively.

TEACHER TIP

RACHEL ZONSHINE, FIFTH GRADE TEACHER (BURBANK, CALIFORNIA)

"I find that when students have choices about where they sit, they are more comfortable and enjoy learning. I have a variety of options where students can sit and work together: wobble stools, bean bags, comfy chairs, benches, cushions, and more. I have collected these over the years and many were free. I also allow students to work in the hallway, which they love. Of course this is a privilege and can be modified if students don't make solid choices.

"I also have a big table in the back of the room where I meet with small groups, and a counter on the side of my room that I use for individual Mastery Checks. I find that area easier to monitor, and it is a clear indicator to all students that students at the counter are taking their Mastery Checks."

Takeaways: Your New Role

In traditional classrooms, teachers drive learning. They deliver live instruction, then tell learners what to do next. Teachers direct; learners follow.

---

[4] To see how Modern Classroom educators in a variety of grade levels and content areas have organized their classrooms, visit www.meeteverylearnersneeds.org.

In a Modern Classroom, your role shifts. You create (or curate) digital direct instruction, then empower students to access your explanations at their own paces. You develop systems for students to work together, then encourage them to learn collaboratively. You're still responsible for designing the learning experience. But your students are responsible for the learning.[5]

And once your digital explanations are clear enough, and your systems for collaboration are strong enough, your lessons will effectively start to run themselves.[6]

MASTERY CHECK

Before advancing to the next chapter, please make sure you understand how to:

☐ Plan opportunities for learners to work together after accessing direct instruction.

☐ Foster a culture of organic collaboration.

☐ Set up your classroom to support group work.

If your class really can run itself, however, you may wonder: what exactly should you, the teacher, do all day? If your students can learn new content from your videos and build understanding from their classmates, what's left for you to contribute?

It's time to sit down with your students.

---

[5] Compared to their peers in traditional settings, students in Modern Classrooms report that they are significantly more likely to learn from their peers during class, and to feel responsible for their own learning. See Wolf, B., Eisinger, J., & Ross, S. (2020). The Modern Classrooms Project: Survey Results for the 2019–20 School Year. Baltimore, MD: Johns Hopkins University.

[6] One unexpected benefit of adopting the Modern Classroom approach was that it became easy for my students to keep learning when I had to miss class. I no longer needed to write detailed sub plans, or hope that substitutes would be able to keep my students engaged: I simply told my students that they'd be responsible for learning whether I was there or not, and asked substitutes to remind my students of that fact. Over the years I received several notes from substitutes who marveled at my students' ability to teach themselves.

Sit Down With Your Students

Digitizing direct instruction makes learning more accessible, facilitates collaboration, and prevents you from repeating the same explanations over and over again. In my opinion, however, the greatest benefit of digital instruction is what it empowers you to do during class.

In a traditional classroom, your ability to work closely with students is limited. Especially at the secondary level, you can spend so much time delivering instruction to your whole class at once that it can be hard to connect personally with any individual learner.

In a Modern Classroom, on the other hand, you no longer need to stand and deliver. Your direct instruction is digitized, so you're free to sit down with individual students or small groups of learners during class. You can engage with each of your learners as a tutor, coach, and mentor. You can work alongside them, rather than policing their behavior from the front of the room.

For most teachers, this newfound freedom is appealing. After all, we become educators because we want to develop meaningful relationships with young people! And sitting down with our learners gives us the time and space to nurture these relationships.

At the same time, abandoning traditional direct instruction can be disorienting. Standing and delivering feels like "what teachers do": it's how we have been trained; it's what we see in movies; and it's often what students, parents, and administrators expect. If you aren't at the whiteboard explaining something or facilitating a whole-group discussion, are you really doing your job?

Fortunately, in a class full of engaged learners with diverse needs, there's still plenty to do.

CHAPTER OBJECTIVES

By the end of this chapter, you will be able to:

1. Build community and have fun with purposeful whole-class activities.

2. Optimize one-on-one interactions through planned check-ins.

3. Deliver small-group mini-lessons for efficiency and collaboration.

You'll still be doing your job, of course—just differently. Teaching doesn't mean lecturing, and the best learning experiences rarely happen when learners sit quietly and take notes. But if you're no longer spending a significant amount of class delivering direct instruction, what should you be doing instead?

My Story: Meeting Students Where They Are

By December, I could keep each of my students appropriately challenged for an entire class period. They would walk in, grab laptops, and watch my video. After watching, they would complete practice problems while I circulated the room to answer questions, then complete an Exit Ticket before leaving class.

My students were more engaged than ever before—and I was happier. I no longer saw David lose interest, rushed Anna through content she struggled to understand, or dreaded Troy's arrival. When students lost focus, I could address them one-on-one, without disrupting the class or losing my cool. I was leaving school every day with my head held high.

Of course there were challenges too. (There always are!) On any given day my students often had more questions than I could possibly answer: even if I spent the whole class running from student to student, I could never seem to reach them all. Some students requested more help than others, which meant I distributed my time unevenly. And while my students happily collaborated with their friends, my classes still lacked a real feeling of community. I wanted every learner to feel as supported as possible, both by me and by their peers.

These were good problems to have. My students had so many questions because they were engaged with the content, I was more available to answer them, and they felt comfortable asking me questions—about math and sometimes about life—one-on-one. The students who demanded more of my attention were just making their needs known. And a calm classroom wasn't a bad thing when I knew that students were working hard and learning. Still, I felt that the class could be more efficient, more equitable, and more engaging for everyone.

In reflecting on these challenges I realized that, despite their varying individual needs, my students had shared needs too. Many had similar gaps in their understanding, so they often got stuck in similar places. Every student, no matter how many questions they asked, deserved my individual attention. And as a whole class, I knew my students would benefit from getting to know one another better. I wanted them to feel like a cohesive group—not just individuals learning on parallel tracks.

So once again, I made some changes. I introduced a whole-class opening routine which I used to build community: I could take this time to review big ideas or make announcements, but we could also use it for icebreakers or math games. I identified the students I spent the most time helping, noted the ones I saw least, and made a concerted effort to distribute my time and attention more equitably. And when I realized that several of my students had similar questions, I saved myself from running around the room by bringing all of those students to me, then addressing those questions in a small-group setting.

These new routines took some time to stick. But once they did, I noticed a real difference. I was getting to know students whom I had previously overlooked, and my students were forming closer relationships as well. The learners who joined my small-group "mini-lessons" spent less time feeling stuck, and I spent less time repeating myself. I noticed a difference in myself, too. I was excited for class to start every day.

When I started at Eastern, my colleagues had encouraged me to "meet students where they are"—in other words, to adapt my instruction to my students' needs. At first I hadn't known how to accomplish that, aside from teaching to the middle. But now I was doing it every day—literally. I was sitting down with every learner and addressing their individual needs.

The ability to work closely with my students during class was my favorite part about teaching in a Modern Classroom. And when I hear from Modern Classroom educators around the world, it's usually what they appreciate most too.

So if you'd like to meet your students where they are—or if you're just wondering how to spend your time in a classroom that effectively runs itself—here's what you can do.

Practice 3.1: Use Whole-Class Time Intentionally

In general, Modern Classroom educators spend much less time teaching whole-class than do traditional teachers. In fact, one of the major benefits of this model is that it replaces stressful whole-class lessons with more productive—and usually more enjoyable—one-on-one and small-group interactions.

With that said, there's still great value in bringing your whole class together at least once per day. Working with your whole class simultaneously can help you:

◆ **Give directions, reminders, and announcements.** Modern Classrooms require students to take ownership of their learning. You can help them succeed by making your expectations clear, then ensuring that every learner knows how to meet them. The most efficient way to do this is often by sharing with your whole class at once.

◆ **Review prior content and big ideas.** You'll cover a lot of content during the school year. It's worth taking time to make sure that your students revisit the things they learned earlier in the year, as well as the overarching themes of your course. Because these reviews will be equally relevant to all of your learners, it's often most efficient to deliver them to the whole class.[1]

◆ **Build community—and have fun!** A Modern Classroom creates the possibility for organic collaboration: when your students aren't sitting quietly listening to you, they can help each other reach mastery. This won't happen, however, unless your students know and feel comfortable around each other. Culture-building activities like games and icebreakers, especially early in the school year, can help foster this kind of cooperation later on. They can also be fun!

---

[1] It is true, of course, that some students will need more review than others—and that absent students will miss out on whole-class review activities. So I recommend that you keep whole-class reviews brief, and that you create self-paced versions that students like Troy can access as well.

In my experience, the best way to give directions, review prior content, and build community is to start each day with a brief whole-class opening routine. You can give your students a warm-up activity to complete together, then spend five to ten minutes reviewing that activity and making announcements. And if you like, you can also end each day with whole-class reflections and/or announcements too.

You may also have certain lessons—complex labs or simulations, structured discussions, seminars, etc.—that work best when the entire class engages simultaneously. In these cases, you should absolutely deliver these lessons to your whole class! There's no need to replace whole-class lessons that work well, and these lessons will feel special to your students when you explain why they are best done collectively. If you do lead this kind of special whole-class activity, I recommend giving students plenty of advance notice, so that they can come to these days of class fully prepared. I also suggest creating self-paced alternatives and/or make-up sessions for students like Troy, who might miss the live lesson but still want to catch up on what was discussed.

Finally, remember that digitizing direct instruction removes some of the time pressure on your class: because students can easily continue to learn outside of class, you don't need to spend every minute in class covering content. So use your whole-class time to have fun! Spending a few minutes each day playing games, doing trivia, or otherwise building community won't prevent your students from learning, but making your class more enjoyable will motivate them to work harder both during and after school.

Ultimately, there's no right or wrong way to use whole-class instruction—and you may find other good uses for whole-group time. As with every aspect of a Modern Classroom, do what works best for you and your learners! Just make sure you're leaving plenty of time for the one-on-one and small-group interactions that your students really need.

TEACHER TIP

DUSTIN TATROE, HIGH SCHOOL ELA TEACHER (BOLINGBROOK, ILLINOIS)

"I start every class together as a full group. We begin with a Do Now and complete our daily check-in. I go over any announcements like office hours, last-call reminders, and upcoming events.

"We also use whole-class time for things like gallery walks or Harkness/Socratic seminars, activities for culture- and relationship-building, addressing common misconceptions, or even reading specific parts of texts together. It is important that scholars always know when those days are coming; otherwise they get frustrated that their self-paced work time is being taken away."

Practice 3.2: Connect With Every Student One-On-One

Whole-class activities can play an important role in your Modern Classroom, but they should no longer be your default form of instruction. Once you finish your opening routine and release your students to watch videos and complete collaborative practice, you'll spend much of your time working one-on-one with your students instead. This feels more like tutoring than like traditional teaching, and it's a lot of fun.

This shift tends to be one of the first things new Modern Classroom educators notice—and one of the changes they enjoy the most. In one-on-one interactions, learners generally feel more comfortable asking questions, and teachers have the time and flexibility to answer them fully. (A ten-minute, whole-class lesson on composite functions might not actually teach any individual student anything, but ten minutes spent answering questions one-on-one certainly will.) There are few things more satisfying than sitting down with a student, answering their questions, and then watching them do something they couldn't do before. And as I'll discuss further in Part 2, these one-on-one interactions also help students and teachers develop meaningful personal relationships, which are both inherently rewarding and powerful motivational tools.

One-on-one instruction in a Modern Classroom happens naturally: you can simply walk around your room and answer questions as they arise. This is good, but keep in mind that the results can be inequitable: the students who feel most comfortable asking questions may receive the bulk of your time, even if other students need it just as much (or more). Responding too quickly to questions, or providing too much assistance, may also prevent your learners from developing their own independent problem-solving skills.

To support all of your students equitably, and foster their independence in the process, I recommend that you:

◆ **Check in with every student regularly, with advance planning if necessary.** You might not be able to sit down with every single learner every single day, but over the course of a few days, you should do your best to connect one-on-one with each of your students. You can track this on a clipboard, or just take a minute at the end of every class to remember whom you did and did not reach.

Some Modern Classroom educators make lists before every class period, with the names of students they want to make sure to check in on. These might be students who need extra help, students who are doing exceptionally well, or students they just haven't spoken with recently. If it will help you connect with every student, I encourage you to make a list too.

◆ **Get on your students' level.** Whenever you can, sit down with your students and talk face to face. This helps students feel valued and respected. It also makes it easier for you to see what they are writing, and where they might be stuck.

◆ **Be intentional about relationship-building.** Every time you answer a question, you have the opportunity to strengthen a personal connection. Take advantage! Figure out what each of your students cares about, then ask about that. Or simply ask, with sincere interest, "How are you today?"

Interactions like these can take ten seconds or less, but they matter. As the saying goes, students won't care how much you know until they know how much you care. And in the event that one of these check-ins takes longer—if, for instance, a student is having a tough day and wants to talk—you'll be there to listen.

◆ **Have an exit strategy.** Your time is limited, and at some point you'll need to go work with other learners too. So once you have answered a student's question and made sure that student knows what to do next, it's time to get out. If the student has more questions, you can direct them to existing resources—back to your video, for instance—or point them in the direction of classmates who might be able to help.

This can be hard in the moment, but it's ultimately in students' best interests: they need to figure out how to answer questions without you there. So be kind, but be firm. You have other students to reach too.

Over time, many Modern Classroom educators note an evolution in the one-on-one support they provide. At first, students ask about the logistics of learning: where to find videos, how to take good notes, what to do next, etc. Once these logistics are familiar, students ask lots of questions about content: they aren't yet comfortable learning from videos and classmates alone. Finally, once students have learned to teach themselves, it's often the teacher who starts asking students the questions, just to check in. If you can get to this point, trust me—it's an amazing place to be.

TEACHER TIP

MEGAN REMMEL, MIDDLE SCHOOL ELA TEACHER (MARRIOTTSVILLE, MARYLAND)

"While my students are self-pacing themselves through my lessons I have the time to sit one-on-one with every student and talk about their writing. I teach language arts, and I've always struggled with finding time to have conversations about individual students' writing, whether it's creative writing or essay writing or a short response, but the Modern Classroom model allows me time to do just that.

"I have now noticed that my students are stepping up their writing because they know that I'm going to sit next to them at some point and have a conversation about their strengths and the things they need to work on. I've noticed that they get really excited when we are talking one-on-one because they get to show me how they have improved and what they have learned in my class this year.

"I never before had the time to look at students' individual needs and address exactly what those individual students need to improve in their writing, but now I have that time and it has made the biggest difference."

Practice 3.3: Plan Small-Group Mini-Lessons

There are inevitably places in your lessons where several of your students will get stuck. They may have common misconceptions or skill gaps; they may encounter a particularly challenging concept or activity; or they may finish a lesson at the same time and need an extra challenge. This is natural, and it presents an opportunity.

When multiple students are stuck in the same place, a small-group "mini-lesson," which addresses the common challenges these students face, can get all these learners unstuck at once. That's more efficient than answering the same questions again and again, and it lets you target all the students who actually need help. A targeted mini-lesson can also spark collaboration between students who are in similar places, strengthening your classroom culture in the process.

To plan an effective mini-lesson:

1. **Anticipate (or identify in real time) common sticking points.** If I'm planning a lesson on composite functions, I can predict that Anna and some of her classmates will need to review function notation, and that David and his peers will finish the lesson quickly and need something challenging to do. I may also notice, in real time, that Troy and a few other students are stuck on problems involving exponents. Each of these situations calls for small-group intervention.

2. **Prepare targeted mini-lessons.** For each sticking point you have identified, develop a short explanation or activity (ideally five minutes or less) that gives struggling students the support they need. You should cover just enough to get students back on track, then move on.

   And while it's nice to plan your mini-lessons in advance, it certainly isn't necessary. If you notice several students struggling with the same concept, just bring them together and help them understand it!

3. **Set aside space.** If you deliver mini-lessons throughout class, it's nice to have a space where students can sit with you and engage. In elementary settings, this might be a carpet or semicircular table; in secondary schools, you can arrange four to eight desks around a whiteboard. If you'd like the ability to deliver

mini-lessons in multiple places, you can also consider getting an easel (with paper or a dry-erase board), or buying whiteboard wall stickers that you can mount around your room. Designating space for small-group instruction creates a more intimate environment, where students can feel comfortable both asking you questions and working collaboratively.

4. **Invite learners to participate.** The value of a focused small-group activity or explanation, aimed at a particular sticking point in a lesson, is that it provides exactly what a handful of students need—while the rest of the class can continue learning independently. It's usually easier to explain something to a small group of learners than to your whole class, too.

So how exactly do you gather the students who need help? I've seen Modern Classroom educators do this in different ways. Some educators identify in advance the students they want to attend each mini-lesson, while others simply announce the mini-lessons they'll deliver that day and encourage students to join those they consider useful.

I recommend that you do both: invite the learners you want to join your mini-lessons, but make these mini-lessons available to any learner who feels they can benefit. This ensures targeted support, while also respecting learner discretion and autonomy. It might also mean that students get up and move around the room to join you, which is a nice way to keep your class dynamic.

And if you do recommend (or require) that certain students attend your small-group mini-lessons, try your best to plan mini-lessons that will eventually reach every learner in your class. While it often makes sense for you to spend small-group time supporting students like Anna and Troy, don't forget that David deserves your attention too. In fact, mini-lessons are great opportunities to challenge your most advanced students! You don't want any of your students feeling singled or left out.

5. **Extend small-group learning through planned collaboration.** When you finish your mini-lesson, you'll now have a group of learners who are sitting together and working on the same thing. This is a great opportunity for collaboration! So at the end of the mini-lesson, point these learners toward a next step they can all take together. If your mini-lesson has been successful, they should be able to support one another in moving ahead while you support the rest of the class.

Effective small-group instruction requires planning and coordination. But it's often more efficient than one-on-one support, and more collaborative too. If you can find a good system for it, both you and your learners will benefit.

TEACHER TIP

LEAH FREDERICK, FOURTH GRADE TEACHER (BELLWOOD, PENNSYLVANIA)

"Every day I use data on student progress to determine which small groups to pull. For example, if I see a group of four learners on Lesson 2 and the rest of the class on Lesson 3, I will know to pull the Lesson 2 kiddos to address misconceptions or give extra practice.

"Most of my learners prefer to work in small groups with their friends to complete assignments. As I am circulating the classroom, I check in with all the groups, typically multiple times per class. Our check-ins involve reflection—'How are these going? What's difficult?'—and a few practice problems with me before I move to the next group."

Takeaways: Giving Learners What They Need

Teaching in a Modern Classroom may feel different from what you and your students are used to. That's a good thing! The traditional approach isn't great for you or for them, while the flexibility of a Modern Classroom lets you respond to each individual learner's needs. It makes teaching more enjoyable for you, too.[2]

And if you're ever unsure what to do in class one day, I encourage you to ask yourself: what does each of your learners really need? If that answer is similar for every student, you can plan a whole-class activity. If there's a smaller group of students who need the same support, it's an opportunity for a mini-lesson. If every

---

[2] Compared to traditional teachers in their schools, Modern Classroom educators were significantly less likely to report that they found class time to be stressful. In fact, only 7% of Modern Classroom educators reported that class time was stressful. See Wolf, B., Eisinger, J., & Ross, S. (2020). The Modern Classrooms Project: Survey Results for the 2019–20 School Year. Baltimore, MD: Johns Hopkins University.

learner needs something different, then you can decide who needs what and provide it one-on-one.[3]

MASTERY CHECK

Before advancing to the next chapter, please make sure you understand how to:

☐ Build community and have fun with purposeful whole-class activities.

☐ Optimize one-on-one interactions through planned check-ins.

☐ Deliver small-group mini-lessons for efficiency and collaboration.

What learners need is what should drive your decisions. And in your Modern Classroom, it will.

Your ultimate goal as a teacher, however, is not just to provide engaging instruction: it's to make sure that your students truly learn. After all, the best-planned and best-delivered lessons aren't worth much if your students can't follow them.

So once you've digitized direct instruction, gotten your learners working together, and figured out how to spend your own time in class, it's time to see what your students understand.

---

[3] If it's helpful, you can use a daily planning template to decide in advance how best to spend class time each day. You can find a downloadable example at www .meeteverylearnersneeds.org.

Require Mastery

To succeed in school—and in life—students must actually under-stand the things they are taught. In other words, they need to achieve mastery.[1]

Mastery matters for two reasons. First, achieving mastery gives young people the foundation of knowledge and skills they need for academic and professional success. David won't become an engi-neer if he can't understand calculus, and at some point Anna's lack of math skills will limit her options for college and/or career. So mastery prepares students for what comes next.

Just as importantly, achieving mastery builds young people's confidence and self-esteem. When we rush students like Anna and Troy through content they aren't prepared to understand, we implicitly teach them that they aren't capable of real learning—and that it doesn't really matter whether they understand or not. When, on the other hand, we require Anna and Troy to achieve mastery, then help them reach it, we send them a powerful message: if you apply yourself, you really *can* learn. The next time they master something, they'll receive that message again; master enough skills, and they'll start to believe it. Once Anna and Troy believe they are capable, there's no limit to what they can learn.

So it's not enough just to keep students in a classroom engaged, or to expose them to new content now in hopes that one day it will make sense. If you're going to teach something, you should make sure your students really understand it.

Unfortunately, most traditional lessons don't require much understanding. In a traditional classroom, David and Anna will progress through the same lessons at the same pace, even if David

---

[1] Some teachers prefer to use terms such as *proficiency* or *competency* here. I use *mastery* because it connotes the high level of skill and understanding of which I believe every young person is capable, but I encourage you to use the term that makes most sense for you and your students.

understands and Anna doesn't. So Anna can sit through a year of math class without ever really understanding anything. By the end of the year, she'll be further behind than when she started. Troy, if he continues to miss class, will be too.

Once you can meet Anna's learning needs, however, you can hold her to a higher standard. When she has the time, support, and resources to understand what functions really are, she actually *can* master composite functions! So can Troy. They can, perhaps for the first time, leave your class with real mathematical understanding— and with pride in their learning too.

Before you can require mastery, however, you need to define what mastery really entails, and how students will demonstrate it. And if you're going to maintain high standards, you also need a plan for when learners fall short.

CHAPTER OBJECTIVES

By the end of this chapter, you will be able to:

1. Administer brief, just-in-time assessments to reveal what learners actually understand.

2. Help learners build mastery through revision and reassessment.

3. Encourage understanding with an efficient and equitable grading policy.

In a Modern Classroom, understanding builds upon itself: what each student understands determines what they should learn next. But how do you know, at any given moment, what each student truly does and does not yet understand? And once you have that information, how can you use it to meet every learner's needs?

My Story: Flipping the Script

Even as I switched from live lectures to digital direct instruction, and from standing at my whiteboard to sitting down with my students, there was one piece of my lesson that remained the same: my daily Exit Ticket. Every day at the end of class, I gave my students a problem to assess their understanding of the day's material.

And while my students were more engaged in class, and I was having more fun, my Exit Tickets still revealed significant gaps between my learners. David, who usually solved all of my practice problems during class, generally showed understanding; Anna, who usually needed more time and support, generally did not. If Troy was absent, he wouldn't take the assessment at all.

The questions on my Exit Tickets weren't bad, but the timing was. There was little point in giving David, at the end of each class, a problem he had already shown he could solve. Nor was it useful for me to give Anna or Troy the same problem when I knew they were not yet ready.

In theory, the results of these Exit Tickets could have helped me plan the next day's lesson. But how? I already knew that David, Anna, and Troy would need different things, so confirming that fact with an Exit Ticket didn't help. Administering and grading the daily Exit Ticket just wasted our time.

Then one day on the way home from school, I had an idea. What if I used the same Exit Ticket questions, but gave them to my students at different times?

I took the next day's Exit Ticket and renamed it: Mastery Check. And when I returned to class, I told my students: "You don't need to take this at the end of class today. Instead, you can take it as soon as you feel ready to succeed."

In that moment, I felt the atmosphere in my room shift. I saw David's face light up: he could take the Mastery Check right away! I saw Anna breathe another sigh of relief: if she needed, she could take it tomorrow. And Troy could take this lesson's Mastery Check whenever he returned to class. Every student could prove their understanding when they felt ready—no sooner and no later.

This system was better for me too: I could now use these just-in-time assessments to require mastery. As soon as David or Anna or Troy demonstrated mastery, they could move on—but if they showed a lack of understanding, I could stop them right then and there. I could send them back to my video for support, or direct them to classmates who had already achieved mastery, or take the time to sit with them and clarify their misconceptions. And then I could let them try the Mastery Check again.

This simple change had profound effects. David no longer had to wait until the next day to begin the next lesson: he could advance as soon as he showed mastery. Anna, if she needed, could spend two days learning the same content, then demonstrate real under-standing as soon as she felt ready. Troy, too, felt supported: when he returned to class, he could start from the first Mastery Check of the unit and move forward from there.

I no longer had to push the class ahead at my one-lesson-per-day pace, regardless of students' understanding. Instead, I could let learners advance at their own paces, and only once they had shown they were ready. And I could use the results of each student's latest Mastery Check to determine that individual student's next steps.

This shift showed each of my learners that, with focused effort and the right support, they really could master precalculus. They could move as fast or as slow as they needed, and develop authentic understanding along the way. And I felt, for the first time in my teaching career, that I could give every learner the support they truly needed—not just to keep them engaged, but also to ensure they understood.

In moving from simultaneous Exit Tickets to just-in-time Mastery Checks, I didn't change the rigor of my assessments. I just changed when I delivered them, and how I responded to the results. I now had real-time data on what my students actually understood, and I could use it to help every student succeed.

Ultimately, the purpose of the Modern Classroom approach is to help every learner achieve mastery. If you're ready to push your own learners toward mastery—and then make sure they reach it—then here's what you can do.

Practice 4.1: Administer Brief, Just-In-Time Mastery Checks

To be useful, the assessments you give students must meet two conditions. First, assessments must be appropriately challenging at the moment when they are given. A question that's clearly too hard or too easy for any individual learner wastes of that learner's time—not to mention your time spent grading it. Second, assessments must provide both you and each learner with clear guidance on that learner's next steps. If your assessments don't, what's the point?

You may already have good assessments planned. But if you assess your whole class at once, you won't appropriately challenge each learner—your questions will be too easy for some and too hard for others—and the results may not clearly indicate what to do next. If half your class shows understanding and the other half doesn't, for instance, whose needs should you prioritize?

For students like David, Anna, and Troy—not to mention their teachers—regular simultaneous assessments (such as daily Exit

Tickets) are rarely worth the time and effort they require.[2] Instead, I recommend that you:

1. Identify questions that cover each of your learning objectives.

2. Give each learner one of these questions when and only when that learner is ready to demonstrate understanding of the objective(s) in question.

I call questions like these, which assess understanding of specific learning objectives at the moments when learners are ready to demonstrate it, Mastery Checks. Mastery Checks show you and each of your students whether or not they have understood a particular lesson's content. And because students take them only when ready—which is what I mean by "just-in-time"—they are always appropriately challenging.

More importantly, Mastery Checks tell you whether or not each of your students should advance to the next lesson. If a student has understood Lesson 1, they should move on to Lesson 2. If not—and if Lesson 1 is worth learning, as all lessons should be—then they should go back and master Lesson 1 first.[3]

I realize, of course, that requiring learners to demonstrate mastery before they advance creates practical complications. In fact, managing those complications is what Part 2 of this book is all about. First, however, I want to explain how you can assess mastery effectively.

To implement just-in-time Mastery Checks with your own learners:

◆ **Cover one learning objective per Mastery Check.** If your Mastery Checks are too frequent or cover too little, you'll be inundated with assessments to review. If your Mastery Checks are too infrequent or cover too much, they'll take longer to review, and they won't provide you or your learners prompt or clear insight into next steps.

---

[2] So long as students care about the results, it can still be useful to administer culminating end-of-unit or end-of-semester assessments, which can inspire students to synthesize their learning and prepare them for high-stakes assessments they may take later in life. But the assessments students take on a more regular basis should always be appropriately challenging, and designed to identify what individual learners should do next.

[3] When a student like Anna fails to understand Lesson 1 of a unit, but moves on to Lesson 2 anyway, she implicitly receives the message that Lesson 1 doesn't matter. If Lesson 1 matters, we should make sure she understands it.

Effective Mastery Checks, therefore, cover a single learning objective; learners in your class should ideally take a new Mastery Check once per day or so. This lets you track and respond to learners' needs without making class an endless stream of assessments.

◆ **Use what you've got.** Creating Mastery Checks from scratch can be a lot of work, so try to find existing questions that cover your learning objectives. If you're not sure where to find questions like these, I suggest looking at school- or district-provided curriculum, or at corresponding questions on standardized year-end assessments.[4] This also keeps your assessments aligned to the specific standards you teach.

◆ **Make Mastery Checks brief and efficient.** The best Mastery Checks contain one or two questions, which you can grade in a minute or less. (The faster, the better.) This helps you focus narrowly on the learning objective in question, and lets you review each learner's work—and determine their next steps—as quickly as possible. Figure 4.1 shows the half-page

Name:	Lesson 1.1: Composite Functions
◎ **Objective: Evaluate composite functions.**	
✎ If $f(x) = 2x^2$ and $g(x) = 3x - 1$, a) Evaluate $f(g(3))$. b) Evaluate $g(f(3))$.	✎ If $f(x) = x^2 + 2$ and $g(x) = x/2$, c) Evaluate $f(g(4))$. d) Evaluate $g(f(4))$.
🏆 **Criteria for Mastery:** Compose all functions in the proper order, and evaluate 3/4 expressions correctly. **Mastered? Circle one:** ☑ **Yes** (advance to next lesson) **/** ☒ **No** (revise practice work, then reassess)	

FIGURE 4.1
A Mastery Check I used for composite functions. It usually took just a few seconds for me to see whether students understood.

---

[4]Many curricula provide Exit Tickets, which can easily be adapted into Mastery Checks. For examples from several popular curricula, visit www.meeteverylearnersneeds.org.

template I used. It was short, simple, and efficient to assess—and it saved paper too![5]

You can also use online platforms to assess learners' understanding, but I prefer paper Mastery Checks for two reasons. First, making students show mastery on paper helps ensure that each student will demonstrates their own understanding: if your Mastery Check is online, a student might get help from a friend or relative at home. This defeats the purpose of Mastery Checks, which is to see what each learner individually understands.

Second, I've found that seeing students' work on paper facilitates feedback. In my experience, automated feedback from a computer just isn't as relatable as feedback delivered with a human touch, and sitting down with a learner over a piece of paper often stimulates better conversation than does looking together at a screen. Taking the time to review Mastery Checks yourself also helps *you* understand where your learners may need extra support.

And if you'd like to try different forms of Mastery Checks, go for it! I'm always in favor of experimentation. I've seen lots of Modern Classroom educators do lots of different things. But I still prefer the simple template in Figure 4.1.

◆ **Outline clear criteria for mastery.** On each Mastery Check, both you and your students should understand: what exactly constitutes mastery for the learning objective in question?

Mastery doesn't require perfection: David can understand composite functions, for instance, and still make calculation errors. But mastery does require that he know how composite functions work. In my math classes, therefore, my Mastery Checks required students to apply the proper problem-solving techniques, even if they made minor mistakes.

You're the expert in your own content area, so you know what real understanding looks like for you.[6] Make that clear to your learners, and you'll set everyone up for success.

---

[5] Necessity is the mother of invention: at Eastern, my colleagues and I had to buy our own paper. In this case, that turned out to be a good thing, as my desire to save paper forced me to make Mastery Checks as efficient as possible. Even at the schools where I taught after Eastern, where I had as much paper as I needed, I continued to use this template.

[6] For real examples of Mastery Checks from a wide range of grade levels and subject areas, please visit www.meeteverylearnersneeds.org.

Finally, once your criteria are clear, you can ask learners to self-assess before starting any new Mastery Check. This is a great exercise for learners, who can reflect on what they do and do not yet understand. Pausing to reflect also increases the chances that learners will demonstrate mastery the first time around: if they aren't yet ready, they can go back and review first.

◆ **Create multiple versions of each Mastery Check.** In a large class, you may have several learners take the same Mastery Check simultaneously. To minimize the risk that students copy from one another, I recommend creating (or finding) multiple versions of each Mastery Check. Having two versions is a good start; if you're able, having three or even four versions is ideal.[7]

Creating multiple versions of each Mastery Check also facilitates reassessment: you can show a student the correct answer to a failed Mastery Check, then give that student another version to try again. I'll discuss this in more detail soon.

◆ **Keep your Mastery Checks organized.** Students should take Mastery Checks as soon as they are ready, so it's important that you and your students can access each Mastery Check as quickly as possible.

When organizing your Mastery Checks, you have a few options. Some teachers prefer to keep Mastery Checks themselves, so that students can't see in advance what questions they'll be asked. These teachers often carry around a folder or binder of Mastery Checks so they always have the right one ready.

Other teachers store Mastery Checks in a place where students can access them independently, as soon as students

---

[7] This won't stop copying altogether, but that's okay. In fact, it creates an opportunity for you to explain the value of academic integrity! If you notice that a student has copied work on a Mastery Check—for instance, if a student is unable to explain the work on their paper—you can take the time to explain why this ultimately hurts the student: copying work prevents that student from developing their own understanding. Then you can simply ask the student to take another version. Personally, I always found this approach much more effective than imposing academic or disciplinary consequences. Students generally know that they aren't supposed to copy, but what they don't often understand is why.

are ready. This means that students can see how they'll be assessed in advance, and take just-in-time assessments without waiting for their teacher.

Other teachers prefer to give Mastery Checks only at specific times. You might let students take Mastery Checks only at the start of each class period, for instance, or only on Tuesdays and Thursdays. This limits the "just-in-time" nature of Mastery Checks, but for good reason: it creates a clear structure, encourages students to be better prepared for each Mastery Check (as their chances to show mastery are limited), and reduces some of the organized chaos that just-in-time mastery assessment can create.

You want Mastery Checks to be efficient, but you also want learners to take them seriously—this will maximize their chances of success, and give you fewer assessments to grade too. (Students will need to reassess less often.) As with all Modern Classroom practices, you should find the option here that works best for you and your learners.

◆ **Ensure individual assessment.** No matter how you design or administer Mastery Checks, it's essential that learners complete these assessments individually. This tells you whether or not each individual student is ready to advance, and prevents any learner from advancing before they are ready.

One way to achieve this is to require that students take their Mastery Checks in the independent-work area of your classroom. Some teachers install dividers between desks to reinforce the importance of individual assessments, while others print Mastery Checks on colored paper. These strategies remind students to complete Mastery Checks independently, and help ensure that students do.

Ultimately, just-in-time Mastery Checks fulfill the real pedagogical purposes of assessment: they tell you what each of your learners actually understands, and give you the information you need to respond accordingly. And because learners take them only when ready, they don't waste anyone's time.

TEACHER TIP

**DEVIN WINTER, FIFTH & SIXTH GRADE TEACHER
(HINESBURG, VERMONT)**

"To create a Mastery Check, I first consider the lesson's objective because I want my Mastery Check to assess that target. Sometimes during this process, it becomes clear to me that I need to break my objective into smaller lesson targets to keep my instructional videos under six minutes.

"I prefer to look at Mastery Checks during class time when possible. That way, I can give my students one-on-one feedback right then and there. When I cannot do it this way, I'll write feedback directly on their Mastery Check so they know what they need to revise. When I feel that a revision requires more than written feedback, I'll write 'R' at the top of their paper and say, 'See me, so we can chat!'

"During the very next class period, I pass back any Mastery Checks submitted the day before. I strategically do this at a time during class when I can meet one-on-one with students who had the 'see me' note on their paper."

Practice 4.2: Require Revision and Reassessment

The results of each Mastery Check should determine each student's next steps. And when students demonstrate mastery, those next steps are clear: advance to the next lesson.

But what if they fall short?

A student who fails to show mastery will likely be disappointed. Yet a failed Mastery Check is, above all, a chance to grow. So rather than letting that student advance with an incomplete understanding (which may come back to hurt them later), you should seize the opportunity to correct the student's misconceptions. Addressing mistakes is how learning happens! And addressing them right away sets learners up for continued success—in your class and beyond.

First, you should diagnose the student's misunderstandings. A good Mastery Check makes this easy: with a quick review, you can see where the student went wrong. You might explain the misconception directly to your student, or make a quick note so that the student can identify it on their own.

Next, the student should revise. In other words, they should revisit the available resources—video, textbook, practice problems, classmates, etc.—and make sure they understand how to complete this Mastery Check correctly. You've identified the misunderstanding, and it's their responsibility to remedy it.

Finally, this student deserves the chance to reassess, using another version of the Mastery Check. (As I mentioned earlier, having multiple versions of each Mastery Check both limits potential cheating and allows for authentic reassessment.) Once a student has revised and feels ready to reassess, they should have the opportunity to prove their understanding again.

This process of developing and demonstrating mastery often requires a mindset shift by students, who may not be used to feeling responsible for their own learning. In traditional settings, in fact, they rarely are: the teacher delivers a lesson, the students apply what they have learned with varying degrees of success, and everyone moves on. But when students must show mastery in order to advance, the dynamic shifts: students become accountable for understanding the material. As I've told many surprised students: "I already know this. Now it's your job to learn it."

To summarize:

1. A student takes a Mastery Check.

2. If the student shows mastery, they advance to the next lesson.

3. If they don't, they:

    a. Return to the lesson and address their mistakes.

    b. Attempt another Mastery Check.

4. And so on, until the student is ready to advance.

It sounds simple enough, and in theory it is. In practice, however, creating smooth systems for revision and reassessment requires careful planning. To make it as smooth as possible, I recommend that you:

◆ **Review completed Mastery Checks ASAP—but avoid bottlenecks.** The outcome of a student's Mastery Check determines what that student should do next, so you'll want to review each student's work as soon as reasonably possible. That way, the student knows whether reassessment is needed—and if so, what resources to use for revision.

With that said, it's not always possible to review Mastery Checks right away, and you don't want students waiting on you. In practice, therefore, you can encourage students to move to the next lesson as soon as they submit each Mastery Check—so long as they are ready to come back, revise, and reassess the previous lesson if needed. Seeing what comes next, even if a student isn't fully ready, won't hurt, but the priority should always be building mastery lesson by lesson. So if a student is working on Lesson 2 when you realize that they failed the Mastery Check for Lesson 1, make sure they revise and reassess on Lesson 1 before continuing on with Lesson 2.

This means that, at a minimum, you should aim to review all submitted Mastery Checks at the end of each day. This will prevent learning gaps from forming, and ensure that each student starts at the right place when they return to class the next day.

◆ **Develop a concrete plan for revision.** Your learners will inevitably need to revise. To make this as smooth as possible, try your best to anticipate common misconceptions, then identify what learners who display those misconceptions can do to clear them up. That way, when a learner needs to revise, you don't need to spend your time re-explaining the concept: you can simply direct the learner to a resource that will help them understand.

For instance, if I'm assessing students on composite functions involving x^3, I'll identify videos students can watch to review both function notation and exponential expressions. That way, if Anna makes a mistake in understanding what $g(2)$ means, she can review function notation; if Troy miscalculates 2^3, he can review exponents. I just need to tell both learners where to look.[8]

---

[8] Given the wide variety of learning gaps that can students bring to class, I wouldn't recommend that you spend time creating your own resources here. That would be too much work! Personally, I created videos for my grade-level content and used YouTube to find videos that helped students review prerequisite content and skills. As I mentioned in Step 1, this both added variety and limited the number of videos I needed to record.

◆ **Have students "earn" reassessments.** Before giving students the chance to reassess, consider asking students to show you—through notes, additional practice, or other evidence of revision—what they have done to prepare. This increases the likelihood that your students will succeed, and keeps your grading workload manageable as a result. Increasing the "cost" of reassessment in this way may also encourage your students to be better prepared the first time around.

◆ **Consider alternate forms of reassessment.** It's possible that some students will struggle to pass your formal Mastery Checks, no matter how many tries they receive. If that happens, you can ask students to demonstrate mastery by explaining their answers orally, creating a visual representation of the content, or sharing what they understand in some other way. Your goal here is to give each learner a fair chance to show you what they know.

In a traditional classroom, learning often becomes a vicious cycle: a student like Anna fails to understand basic skills yet moves to more advanced content regardless, where she is even less prepared to succeed. Her learning gaps grow wider over time, and she falls further and further behind.

Revision and reassessment of Mastery Checks, however, turn this paradigm on its head. The requirement that learners show mastery—combined with the processes of revision and reassessment whenever they fall short—prevents learning gaps from forming in the first place. So the learning cycle becomes virtuous: students' mastery of basic skills prepares them to master more and more complex content. This way, learners in Modern Classrooms are always working on content they are prepared to understand. And every learner has the opportunity—and the support—to achieve real mastery.[9]

---

[9] Compared to their peers in traditional classrooms, students in Modern Classrooms are significantly more likely to report that they can complete challenging assignments without giving up and that they really understand what they are learning. See Wolf, B., Eisinger, J., & Ross, S. (2020). The Modern Classrooms Project: Survey Results for the 2019–20 School Year. Baltimore, MD: Johns Hopkins University.

TEACHER TIP

WILLIAM BRADSHAW, HIGH SCHOOL CAREER & TECHNICAL EDUCATION TEACHER (REIDSVILLE, NORTH CAROLINA)

"I no longer just issue percent grades and move on. Instead I provide feedback, and if a student's work is below mastery level, they must resubmit.

"I'm finding that my students are learning more with my guidance and that they also don't want their work to be returned the first time. What ends up happening is that the quality of their work increases the first time around, so I'm more often able to say 'Hey, this is fantastic, move on to the next activity!'"

Practice 4.3: Use Grades to Emphasize Mastery

Assessing students' understanding raises a question that is never far from either teachers' or students' minds. When mastery is assessed, how should it be graded?

Grading, especially at the secondary level, presents all sorts of philosophical questions. Should grades reflect students' effort or understanding? Should grades count all of a student's work equally, or should recent assignments receive greater weight? Should grades be used as a tool to motivate learners, or are they simply a representation of how a student has performed?

I don't know your answers to these questions, nor do I know your students or your school's policies. Besides, different Modern Classroom educators have different approaches to grading. So I don't feel comfortable recommending a particular grading policy.

If you're going to run a Modern Classroom, however, you'll probably need to figure out how grades fit in. And while I don't believe there's a single right way to grade in a Modern Classroom, I do think there are a few principles you can use to align your grades with both the principles and the practices of mastery. In applying these principles, you can emphasize to your students why mastery really matters—and make your own life easier too.

No matter how or what you grade, I encourage you to:

◆ **Grade what really matters.** Teachers often try (or are required) to grade everything students do. Not only does this create a lot of work, but it also fosters in students a mindset that what matters is simply completing each assignment. The teacher gives tasks, and students accumulate points. There is little focus on what really matters—just a constant push to get work done.

When I was teaching, I saved myself time—and emphasized the importance of mastery—by grading only learners' Mastery Checks, as well as larger end-of-unit assessments. I didn't grade my students' notes, practice problems, or participation: the purpose of all these activities was simply to prepare learners for Mastery Checks. Students soon understood what I cared about: not just that they did the work, but rather that they understood the content.

For the same reason, I also did not assign homework. My lessons contained everything my students needed to achieve mastery, and it didn't matter to me whether they developed understanding in class or at home. If students wanted to work after class, I encouraged them to—and my videos made this easy. But ultimately, there was no difference between the work they did in class and what they could do at home. It was all just preparation for Mastery Checks and end-of-unit assessments.

Depending on your school's policies, you may or may not be able to reduce your grading load—or eliminate formal homework—the way I did. Or you may not want to! If you can focus on grading what matters, however, you can make both your and your students' lives easier.

◆ **Encourage reassessment.** If we want students to revisit and learn from their mistakes, we can't penalize them for doing so. Much as I want students to do work promptly and accurately the first time around, I believe that policies like late-work penalties and partial credit for reassessments harm students more than they help. True learning can't be scheduled, and falling short the first time is an inevitable—and important—part of any student's learning experience.

In my class, therefore, I gave students unlimited opportunities to retake Mastery Checks—provided that they showed evidence of preparedness, and using new versions of each Mastery Check every time—then awarded full credit when they ultimately achieved mastery.

◆ **Focus on feedback.** It's good to tell students whether they have shown mastery, but it's much better to give students actionable feedback that helps them grow. Too often, when we have stacks of papers to evaluate, this is the part of grading that gets lost.

If you're grading less, however, and emphasizing mastery, you can take the time to provide meaningful feedback on each learner's work. Because you'll return Mastery Checks to individual students as students complete them (rather than returning a whole stack of identical assessments at once), you should have the time and flexibility to tell each learner, after each Mastery Check, what they did well and where they can do better. Even a fifteen-second check-in can make a big difference in a student's understanding. It can also help you strengthen your relationship with that young person.

These principles—like everything else in this book—are just my recommendations. You can and should adapt (or ignore) them as best meets your and your students' needs! But if you can bring these principles to life in your own classroom, you'll place the focus of your and your students' time and energy where it should be: on mastery. You'll create the conditions for true learning to occur. And once you can do that within a single lesson, you can do it every day.

TEACHER TIP

ELLEN GAMMEL, STEM INSTRUCTIONAL COACH (FITCHBURG, MASSACHUSETTS)

"Students are starting to truly see that grades are about learning, not just numbers in a gradebook. At first students who did not reach an 85% on the Mastery Check said, 'Why didn't I get an 85?' But after about a month, I now hear students say, 'I didn't reach mastery yet, but I figured out what I did wrong, so can I try again?' They're starting to understand that their grades reflect their learning. Now, students really care that they are learning."

Takeaways: Seeing the Bigger Picture

I hope at this point the requirement of mastery—and the entire structure of a typical Modern Classroom lesson—makes sense. A student watches your video, takes notes, works collaboratively with classmates, gets your help as needed, and attempts a Mastery

Check when ready.[10] If the student shows mastery, they repeat that sequence for the next lesson; if not, they revise and reassess until they are ready to advance. In lessons like these, students as diverse as David, Anna, and Troy can all be appropriately challenged—and appropriately supported too. And once you require mastery, they'll all start to acquire it.

MASTERY CHECK

You've almost finished Part 1 of this book! Before advancing to the next chapter, please make sure you understand how to:

- ☐ Administer brief, just-in-time assessments to reveal what learners actually understand.
- ☐ Help learners build mastery through revision and reassessment.
- ☐ Encourage understanding with an efficient and equitable grading policy.

Lessons like these help every learner succeed. Yet most lessons exist within larger units, which exist within larger courses. And while providing students the time and support they need to reach mastery makes sense at the lesson level, it quickly becomes complicated when you consider all the content you need to teach in a year.

If, for instance, David works ahead while Anna builds prerequisite skills and Troy catches up, how can you ensure that they all cover the same year's worth of content? If different students are working on different things at the same time during class, how does each learner know what to do? And how do you, as a teacher, manage it all?

These are excellent questions—I encountered them as well—and I'm excited to answer them. Once you've redesigned your lessons, you're ready to start redesigning your courses too.

---

[10] This gradual release strategy resembles the "I Do, We Do, You Do" approach: the teacher explains on video, then students practice together, then students take Mastery Checks individually. Videos, however, make instruction more accessible than in traditional classrooms, and just-in-time Mastery Checks ensure that learners are always prepared to succeed.

And while this is a logical structure, remember that you don't need to follow it exactly. As I wrote in Step 2, you can also foster inquiry and productive struggle by giving students practice tasks *before* they watch your videos. Do what works best for you!

Part 2

Redesigning Courses

Seeing David, Anna, and Troy master my lessons felt great. I was having fun in class now, and they were too.

But I had another problem. My students were achieving mastery at different rates.

David liked learning fast, but he finished fast too. Anna liked having the time she needed, but she always needed more. Troy liked being able to catch up, but it was hard for him to do that when he wasn't in class.

So at the end of each lesson, I found myself in a familiar predicament. David wanted more to learn. Anna had too much. I wasn't sure when I would see Troy next. I had a lot of content to cover, but limited time in which to cover it.

My redesigned lessons were a good start. But I needed those lessons to fit smoothly together, so that David could push ahead, Anna could persevere, and Troy could pick up wherever he had last left off. And I needed to ensure that, by the end of the school year, all three students would cover the key points of precalculus.

If I wanted to meet every learner's needs, in other words, I needed to redesign my whole course too.

The Challenge of Courses

Time may give our lives meaning, but it sure makes teaching hard.

Given unlimited time, any person can learn anything. But our time with our students is limited, and we have lots of content to cover. So we divide the courses we teach into units, then lessons, then individual activities, each with its own allocation of time. And in order to "get through all the content"—a joyless phrase I often hear educators use—we move students from lesson to lesson, at the teacher's pace, even when students don't understand. If we want to cover everything, what other choice do we have?

In a Modern Classroom, of course, you can remove the time constraints on individual lessons. You can digitize direct instruction and give each learner the time—and the support—they need to reach mastery.

But you can't rewrite your curriculum, nor escape a larger school system in which your students are expected to encounter a predefined amount of material by the time they graduate. Your students, in other words, still need to get through all the content. And if your class is fully self-paced, there's no guarantee they will.

There is, therefore, a fundamental tension between the fact that students have different needs and the design of our time-bound education system. And when you launch a Modern Classroom, you're caught squarely in the middle. How can you possibly give every learner both a full course of content and the time they actually need to master it all?

I believe there is a way. I believe that if you prioritize your content, design systems that support self-paced learning, and find ways to motivate your students, you really can help every learner master every key concept of the course(s) you teach. That's what I'll teach you to do in Part 2 of this book.

Before I do that, however, I want to clarify the challenge. I want to describe the pressure I felt to cover content, explore how that made my students feel, and explain why it's unreasonable to expect that every student in a traditional course will learn the exact same amount of content in a given school year. Once you understand those things, you'll be ready to make the compromises that meeting every learner's needs, in a one-size-fits-all system, ultimately requires.[1]

CHAPTER OBJECTIVES

By the end of this chapter, you will be able to:

1. Articulate the challenges posed by traditional year-long courses.

2. Empathize with students who are unable to achieve their full potential in time-bound courses.

3. Define the characteristics of a course that meets every learner's needs.

If we want all students to succeed, we need to teach them lots of things. We also need to give them the time they need to learn. Here's why traditional courses make it impossible to do both.

My Dilemma

I began giving just-in-time Mastery Checks in January, at the start of my unit on trigonometry. I watched with pride as my students began to achieve mastery. David, Anna, and Troy positively beamed with it.

But I had a problem. Three days in, David was already on Lesson 4. Anna had worked hard but needed significant remediation; after several attempts, she had just mastered Lesson 1. And Troy hadn't shown up yet. So I looked at my calendar—I had planned to spend three weeks on this particular unit—and realized that David might finish two weeks early, Anna might not reach the end, and Troy might not even get started.

I certainly didn't want to slow David down. But I didn't want to rush Anna or Troy either: pushing them to finish the unit without

---

[1] As I'll discuss in Part 3, the problem here is really our age-based education system: when we advance students from grade to grade based on age instead of understanding, it's inevitable that students with different needs will learn different amounts. But when you've got a class of diverse learners in front of you, it won't do you much good to worry about this—at least not until your Modern Classroom is up and running. Your immediate goal is to meet those students' day-to-day learning needs.

understanding it would only make things worse. And while I encouraged Anna and Troy to keep learning after class, using my videos for guidance, I wasn't sure whether they had the support at home to do that successfully.

I felt stuck. I wanted to give each student the time they needed to master the entire unit, but I still had several more units to teach—and only so many days left in the school year. I couldn't give Anna or Troy more time to master trigonometry without sacrificing other content, and I couldn't teach them more content without cutting into their mastery of trigonometry. Was it better for Anna and Troy to see a full year's worth of content they could only partially understand, or to fully understand only part of my course's content?

I also didn't know what to do about David, who was on track to finish my remaining units in half the time I'd initially planned. It didn't seem fair to limit him to the content of the syllabus alone. On the other hand, I had no idea how to give him more when Anna and Troy were already overwhelmed.

I had students who were on track to finish early, students who needed more time to learn, and a syllabus with no room to spare. What could I do?

One Pace Fits None

We know, as educators and as human beings, that people learn at different paces. This is true when our students start learning a new skill, like trigonometry, at the same time. It's even more pronounced when our students come to those skills with varying levels of confidence and background knowledge, and when some students attend class more often than others. The idea that any diverse group of learners will learn the exact same amount of content in the exact same amount of time is unreasonable.

Yet this idea drives our entire school system. A fifth-grade English teacher, for instance, starts the school year with a certain amount of content their students are expected to cover. The fifth-grade curriculum is based on what we assume students have learned in fourth grade (and grades prior), and the curriculum for sixth grade (and grades beyond) is based on what we assume students will learn in fifth grade. It doesn't matter if a student like David has shown that he already understands all of what fifth grade will cover, or if a student like Anna has shown minimal understanding of fourth-grade content, or if a student like Troy misses half the school year. The fifth-grade curriculum is the fifth-grade curriculum, and—because students will move to sixth grade next year—the teacher must teach it.

So it's not just lessons that get taught to the middle—it's whole courses too. We can never fully make it through curricula intended for students with grade-level skills, because so many of our students are behind. (Remember, most American fourth-graders are considered below proficient in reading.) In covering as much as we feel we can, however, we inevitably leave slower-moving learners even further behind. We fail to challenge David, who could learn the full curriculum and more, yet we advance much too fast for Anna and Troy to keep up. One-size-fits-all doesn't work for lessons, and it doesn't work for courses either.

I think it's possible to redesign courses in the same way that we can redesign lessons, so that every student is appropriately challenged and supported every day. But first I want to emphasize why it's necessary.

How Courses Feel

In theory, giving all students rigorous, on-grade-level instruction is a noble goal.[2] Every student should have the opportunity to learn all of the content and skills that we deem valuable for college and career! I empathize with educators, administrators, and policymakers who set high expectations for the rigor and quantity of content their students will cover.

In practice, however, I think we do our students a disservice when we give them content which we know they are not yet prepared to master—or which they have already shown they understand. When we ask learners with different needs to learn the

---

[2] As I'll discuss in Part 3, the age-based concept of being "on grade level" is itself problematic: why should we expect every ten-year-old, regardless of background knowledge or circumstances, to learn the exact same things? If my kid has second-grade math skills, I want him to learn third-grade math next—no matter how old he happens to be! But I use "on grade level" here because it's a phrase I hear a lot, and because it's a useful shorthand for the idea that, in our current system, students at a particular age are all expected to understand a particular set of skills.

same quantity of content in the same amount of time, it's inevitable that:

◆ **Students like David, who are proficient or advanced, won't have enough to do.** My precalculus syllabus contains a list of topics I plan to cover over the course of the school year. But David, who learns quickly, doesn't need a full year to learn them all. Now that he's moving at his own pace, I'm confident he can master the rest of precalculus by March.

I suppose this is a good problem to have. But even if David finishes early, he'll still need to come to class, and I don't know what he'll actually do there: I don't have the time to create entire calculus units specifically for him. But I also don't want him just sitting around: that would create a classroom-management challenge, and it wouldn't be fair to David either. I want him to learn as much as possible, but there are limits to how much I can teach.

◆ **Students like Anna, who are far behind, will fall even further behind.** Anna now has the time she needs to learn—but she needs more time than my year-long course allows. After all, she has remediation to do first! The content of my precalculus course is meant for students with grade-level skills, and Anna's skills lag several years behind. Realistically, there's no way she can catch all the way up, while simultaneously learning a full year's worth of precalculus, in the one year we have together.

Anna, unfortunately, is used to this: she was behind after fourth grade, fell further behind in fifth grade, and has continued to fall further behind every year since. She has always managed to pass—her teachers don't want to hold her back—and, with one more math credit standing between her and graduation, I'll probably find a way to pass her too.[3] But

---

[3] When it comes to grading, it's very difficult to hold students like Anna to grade-level expectations. It's not Anna's fault that she has been put in ever-more-advanced math courses without prerequisite skills, and it's not clear what failing her—thus requiring her to retake classes she wasn't prepared for in the first place—would accomplish. So teachers like me pass her and her classmates along anyway. Of the students I taught at Eastern, for instance, only 1% were ever proficient in Algebra 1, but somewhere around 70% always graduated. I was as complicit here as anyone else.

math feels less and less accessible every year, while Anna feels more and more inadequate.

In my class Anna feels newfound confidence—for the first time in her life, she's actually mastering grade-level math!—but she still feels hopeless. Even if she masters some of my content, there's inevitably more she won't reach. By the end of the year, she may be even further behind.

◆ **Students like Troy, who are chronically absent, may give up altogether.** My precalculus syllabus doesn't work particularly well for David or Anna, but for Troy it's a disaster. If I don't have enough time to cover all my content with the students who are in class every day, how can I possibly do that with a student who's late or absent much of the time? Without significant help outside of class, which I know Troy doesn't have, he can't possibly learn a year's worth of content in half a year's worth of school.

Digitized direct instruction and self-paced lessons give Troy some hope: he can walk into my class, pick up where he left off, and achieve mastery. Yet when he comes back to school after a prolonged absence, he also sees how much further he now has to go. Like Anna, he feels both inspired and discouraged. Hard as he tries, he just can't seem to catch up.

I was proud to see David, Anna, and Troy engage and achieve mastery, but I felt stressed too. I knew that these learners were all capable of understanding precalculus—and more—if they had the time, yet I only had so much time to give. I didn't want David to run out of content, and I didn't want Anna or Troy to feel constantly overwhelmed.

So while my individual lessons met these learners' needs, the design of my entire precalculus course didn't. At least not yet.

Toward Better Courses

Time is always limited, and there's a lot that we want young people to learn. So we divide human knowledge into discrete chunks we call courses, allocate to each of those courses a fixed amount of time, and hope that our students will understand as much of each course as reasonably possible in the time provided. This system seems both efficient and equitable: today, every young person in the United States will see roughly the same content by the time they turn eighteen (if they don't drop out first). In some way, that's actually pretty amazing.

When we remember that every learner is different, however, we should realize that expecting every student to learn the same amount of content in the same amount of time is neither equitable nor efficient. It's the rigidity of this system that forces teachers to give students like Anna content for which they are obviously unprepared, while preventing students like David from advancing as far or as fast as they could go. And it leads to both David and Anna—not to mention millions of other young people—wasting years of their youth in courses that fail to meet their needs. One-size courses fit none.

It's worth asking, therefore: what's the alternative? What kind of courses would unlock each of these young people's full potential, and make good use of their precious time in the process? In a better course:

◆ **David would have ample opportunity to deepen his understanding.** Any topic can be extended in different and interesting directions. Rather than limiting him to the content of the syllabus, a truly effective course would let David go further along the paths that most interest him.

◆ **Anna would learn the essentials first.** In every course, there are things that students truly *need* to know, along with things that are nice to know. The syllabi I've seen rarely distinguish these things—but we as teachers should. If Anna isn't able to master every single piece of content in the time she has in class, she should at least be able to focus on the things that really matter.

◆ **Troy would have a legitimate chance to master everything.** It's too easy for Troy to give up: he has too much to learn, and too little time in which to learn it. So what Troy needs, more than anything, is to feel that if he applies himself in class—and potentially outside of class too—he can actually succeed. If he really believes that, there's a good chance he will.

Perhaps most importantly, each of these learners should have— regardless of their current progress through the course—a clear and efficient path toward full understanding. At any given point in the course, in other words, they should know exactly what comes next—and what they can do to master it. Our young people's time is far too valuable to waste.

MASTERY CHECK

Before advancing to the next chapter, please make sure you understand how to:

☐ Articulate the challenges posed by traditional year-long courses.

☐ Empathize with students who are unable to achieve their full potential in time-bound courses.

☐ Define the characteristics of a course that meets every learner's needs.

Courses like the ones I've just described may sound impossible to create. They aren't. They begin with a change of pace.

Step 5

Help Learners Set the Pace

Students need different amounts of time to understand new content. Teachers have fixed amounts of time and content to teach. Something's got to give.

In a traditional classroom, it's student understanding that suffers. The bell rings, class ends, and the teacher delivers Tuesday's lesson whether students understood Monday's lesson or not. There's a syllabus to get through, and the teacher just has to keep moving. Learning gaps form and grow wider over time.

In a Modern Classroom, where students can access instruction and demonstrate mastery at their own paces, students now have the time they need to learn. But this creates challenges too. A student like Anna may need a week to understand content that was scheduled to take a day, and a student like David may understand in a day content that was scheduled to take a week. If you just let them set their own paces all year, David may finish your syllabus in December, and Anna may never finish. This isn't great either.

As a teacher, therefore, you need a way to give Anna more time, and give David more challenge, while somehow ensuring that both learners—and all their classmates—cover the key points of your course. You need to balance structure with autonomy, equity with equality, and the needs of your students with the demands of your content.

In other words, you need to compromise.

CHAPTER OBJECTIVES

By the end of this chapter, you will be able to:

1. Set appropriate intervals for self-paced learning.

2. Prioritize content by classifying learning activities.

3. Balance the needs of your learners with the demands of your curriculum.

This is, perhaps, the fundamental challenge of the Modern Classroom. How can you cover all the content you're supposed to cover while simultaneously giving each learner the time they need to reach mastery? And if your students learn at different paces, but you have the same amount of time with all of them, how can you push each individual learner to master as much as they possibly can?

My Story: Mind the Gaps

Moving from simultaneous Exit Tickets to just-in-time Mastery Checks was a huge step for me. Within any given lesson, my students now had the time they needed to achieve real understanding. David could move as fast as he wanted, and I no longer felt the need to rush Anna or Troy along. Every student could now reach mastery, and I could support them all.[1]

It wasn't long, however, before the gaps between my learners started to grow. David soon reached the end of my unit, while Anna and Troy remained near the beginning. The other twenty learners in my class were all spread throughout. All of my students were engaged, which was good. But my job was to teach an entire precalculus course—and at this rate, there was no way they were all going to master all of it.

I briefly considered returning to my traditional approach, which would have ensured we covered everything. But David would have been bored, Anna's head would have been down on her desk, and Troy would have been lost the moment he arrived. After all the progress we'd made, that didn't feel right.

I also considered just letting my students advance at their own paces for the rest of the year. But I realized that if my students eventually became spread across multiple units, it would be harder for me to facilitate engaging whole-class activities or small-group mini-lessons, and harder for my students to collaborate with peers

---

[1] In a traditional classroom, teachers differentiate instruction in terms of content: within a fixed amount of time, students receive different amounts or degrees of content. In a typical "low-floor, high-ceiling" task, for instance, David will work on harder problems than will Anna, and they'll both move to the next task at the same time. In a Modern Classroom, on the other hand, teachers provide all students with equally rigorous content—what differentiates students is the time they take to learn it. In a Modern Classroom, therefore, every learner can reach the ceiling.

learning similar content. I also feared that, if Anna and Troy continued to move slowly, they would never reach the units I had planned toward the end of the year. I thought these units were valuable and wanted all my students to see them. So that wasn't a great option either.

I knew that, to achieve mastery, my students needed to learn at their own paces. Yet I also wanted to facilitate collaboration and small-group instruction, while ensuring that every student could master the key content of my course. So I made two compromises.

- ◆ **I let my students set their own paces—but only within defined intervals.** I told my students, for instance, that they would have three weeks to work on my trigonometry unit, but that once those three weeks were finished, we would all start fresh on the next unit. I also created suggested deadlines for each of my lessons, so that students could assess their own progress against my recommended pace.

  This was, I admit, stressful for learners like Anna and Troy: they knew they'd be under pressure to finish the unit in time. But it created clarity around my expectations, as well as a healthy sense of urgency. Anna and Troy could still take the time to build mastery step-by-step, from my first lesson to the last, but they now had a clear and achievable endpoint in sight. They felt motivated to reach it. And if they didn't quite reach the last few lessons in time, they could always go back and master them later, using my videos for support. This wasn't ideal, but I didn't see any other way to help them understand all the key concepts of precalculus.

- ◆ **I prioritized within the curriculum itself.** I knew that, given the differing skills my learners brought to class, David would be able to cover more than Anna and Troy would. So rather than ignoring this fact, I embraced it. I higlighted the truly essential content that I expected every learner to master—my "Must-Do" content—and classified everything else as "Should-Do" or "Aspire-to-Do." In other words, I made sure that Anna and Troy could focus first and foremost on the core content of precalculus, while creating opportunities for David to extend his understanding with rich extension tasks.

I let my students set their own paces, but with clear guideposts and within reasonable intervals. My students' job was simply to learn as much as they could before each end-of-interval assessment. My typical self-paced interval looked something like Figure 5.1.

Unit 5: Trigonometric Functions

Lesson	Priority	Suggested Due Date
5.1: Sine and Cosine Functions	Must-Do	January 5
5.2: Function Transformations	Must-Do	January 7
5.3: Sinusoidal Models	Must-Do	January 11
5.4: Tangent Functions	Should-Do	January 13
5.5: Inverse Trig. Functions	Aspire-to-Do	January 15
5.6: Trig. Functions Review	Should-Do	January 19

Trigonometric Functions Test: January 21

FIGURE 5.1

An example of a full self-paced interval in my classroom, with lessons classified by priority and suggested due dates.

This was an important shift in my practice, so there are three things worth noting here.

1. According to my suggested pace, students typically had two days to complete each lesson. There's no reason that students should be expected to master a self-paced lesson within exactly one class period.

2. My self-paced intervals usually began with Must-Do content, then had Should-Do and Aspire-to-Do lessons toward the end. I knew that Anna and Troy might only complete Lessons 1–3, which were the most important. I also knew that David could push himself to master all six lessons.

3. All my students took an end-of-interval assessment on the same day. This created accountability and urgency, as well as a natural "reset point" after the test. My test covered mostly Must-Do content, but it did have a few questions about the Should-Do and Aspire-to-Do material as well: this rewarded students who had gone further and also gave students like Anna the chance to tackle new problems.[2] After the test, my class would start fresh with a new unit on a new topic—although students were always free to go back, on their own time, to master lessons they had not yet finished.

These compromises were not perfect. Anna and Troy still struggled to master all of my Must-Do content, and David wasn't always convinced that the "extra" work was worth his effort.

On the whole, however, my prioritized, self-paced units worked much better than the traditional, teacher-led units I'd been trained to deliver. I was covering the same amount of content, but:

◆ **My expectations for self-paced learning were clear.** My students were free to learn at their own paces, but they knew every day where I wanted them to be. Suggested deadlines for each lesson created urgency as well. Students in my class may have fallen behind my suggested pace, but they never wasted time feeling lost.

◆ **Students felt ownership of their learning.** Within any self-paced interval, my students were responsible for how much they understood. My job was simply to guide them toward mastery.

◆ **Students spent their time where it mattered most.** My students knew what was truly essential to master, and they also knew how to extend themselves beyond the basics once they were ready.

◆ **Students were always able to collaborate.** Even if students were at different points within my self-paced intervals, they were still always learning the same general topics. This made working together both natural and productive—especially when students who were ahead of my suggested pace could help their classmates catch up.

---

[2] It might seem unfair to Anna to include assessment questions on content she hadn't yet reached during class. I don't think it is: despite the challenges she faces, Anna has had as much time to access the Should-Do and Aspire-to-Do content as anyone else. In fact, you might be surprised at how often a student like Anna, who has developed a real understanding of Must-Do content, can make progress on more advanced questions during a test even if she hasn't yet reached those topics in her lessons. And it sure beats the traditional approach, in which Anna must take a test on a whole bunch of content she only partially understands.

◆ **Students could always catch up.** Even if learners couldn't master everything by the end of a given self-paced interval, they could go back and watch my videos later. Before I started using videos, students like Troy had no real way to catch up. Now, they did.

Balancing my learners' needs with my curriculum's demands was always a challenge: I wanted my students to learn all of precalculus, and I also wanted them to learn each skill deeply! The compromises I made were never perfect. But at the end of each self-paced interval, I knew I had given each of my students the best opportunity I could to master that interval's content.

Finding the right balance here may be challenging for you too, as it has been for thousands of other Modern Classroom educators. But if you're ready to foster deep understanding while covering everything you must cover, here's what you can do.

Practice 5.1: Set Appropriate Intervals

If you don't give your students the time they need to reach mastery, they won't achieve it. If you give them too much flexibility, however, you may sacrifice urgency. And the longer you allow students to go before a whole-class reset, the larger the gaps between learners can grow.

I recommend, therefore, that you define intervals of time during which students can learn at their own paces. At the start of each interval, all students begin at the same place; at the end of each interval, there is a clear goal toward which all students aim. This creates clarity and urgency, gives students regular chances to start fresh, and facilitates collaboration by ensuring that all students in your class are working within the same set of lessons.

This can be an uncomfortable compromise: a student like Troy might only be halfway through a given interval's content when you move on to the next one. But within each interval, that student can now build mastery step-by-step, instead of seeing only the lessons you happen to teach on the days he's in class.[3] Besides, your digital

---

[3] Imagine a five-lesson sequence that occurs over the course of a week—Lesson 1 on Monday, Lesson 2 on Tuesday, etc.—and say that Troy makes it to class only on Wednesday and Friday. In a traditional classroom, Troy would see Lessons 3 and 5, neither of which is likely to make much sense out of context. In a Modern Classroom, however, Troy can start on Wednesday with Lesson 1, make as much progress as possible from there, and catch up on the rest later.

direct instruction remains available when he wants to go back and master lessons he has missed. So it's the best compromise I've found.

The intervals you choose for self-paced learning depend on your and your learners' needs; as with every Modern Classroom practice, you know your learners (and yourself) best, so do what works for you! As you determine how to set these intervals, I recommend that you:

◆ **Start small.** Let learners work at their own paces for a day or two, then reset. If that feels too rushed, make the next interval longer; if not, stick with relatively short intervals. Your students will become more and more comfortable with self-paced learning over time, so don't give them too much freedom until they are ready for it.

Personally, I found that two-to-three week intervals worked well for my precalculus students: once they were comfortable learning at their own paces, that duration gave them meaningful autonomy without letting the gaps grow too wide. But it took us time to get there—and what worked for my teenagers may not work for your students. In fact, some of the most effective Modern Classroom educators have students learn at their own paces for just a few days at a time. And many start, as I initially did, by self-pacing only within each day of class, then starting fresh with a new lesson the next day.

I've learned over the years that students can easily get lost—and fall hopelessly far behind—in a self-paced interval that's too long, but that they'll rarely mind a window that feels short. (After all, most students aren't used to any self-pacing at all.) So start small.

◆ **Set suggested deadlines within intervals—and firm ones at the end.** No matter how long your intervals for self-paced learning, it's helpful for students to know exactly where you expect them to be. This creates urgency, and helps students understand whether they are on- or off-track to succeed. These deadlines may only be suggestions—students can and should progress at their own paces—but they are helpful guideposts.

I recommend, however, that your deadlines for the end of each interval be firm. This creates accountability for learners: when the interval ends, you all move on. Students can always go back and access past lessons on their own time anyway.

And whatever your deadlines, make sure they are clearly posted so that students are always aware.

◆ **Teach time management explicitly.** Taking ownership of their learning may be new to students who are used to following along at their teacher's pace. So in addition to being clear about what your students should be doing in class, you should take the time to explain how they can be most successful.

In particular, you should teach them how to manage their time during class, and how they can take advantage of additional support—from you, classmates, families, etc.— once class ends. This will set your students up for success in your class, and better prepare them for life afterward too.

◆ **Provide learners room to fail.** The most valuable lesson I ever taught my students wasn't about math. It was that if they applied themselves, they could succeed—and that if they wasted time they should have spent working, they might fail.

At the start of the year, my students often did waste time—and their early grades reflected that. This was painful for all of us, but my students learned from it. They came to understand that success in my class was ultimately a matter of effort, and that with enough effort, each of them could succeed. By my third self-paced interval, my students were much more focused than they'd been during my first. And by the end of the year, every student understood that they were responsible for—and capable of—their own success.

◆ **Make it easy for students to catch up later.** Unfortunately, it's inevitable that some students will fail to reach all of the content in each of your intervals. But that doesn't mean they can't learn it later! If your direct instruction is digitized, they can always catch up when they have time, whether that's in school, at home, or anywhere else they can access the Internet.

At the end of each self-paced interval, therefore, I recommend that you remind students where they can go to find the lessons they have missed. (I'll discuss how you can organize digital content in the next chapter.) That way, students can still master everything you want them to learn.

And if your students have missed content from a previous unit, they should never be bored in class: they can always go back and catch up! If I ever had a spare day of class—during standardized testing, for instance, or around school events that disrupted my regular schedule—I always had a plan for my students: they could simply revisit prior lessons they had missed. This was an easy way for me to keep my students engaged, and a good use of their time and attention.

Setting appropriate intervals is a balancing act, and you may not get it right the first time. That's okay! You'll learn and adjust. The key is to give your students control over their learning, as well as the opportunity to fail, without providing more freedom than they are prepared to handle.

And no matter how small your intervals of self-paced learning, or how clear your deadlines and directions, your learners may still struggle with their newfound autonomy. That's also okay! Stick with it. As your students become comfortable pacing themselves, which they eventually will, they'll become more independent, self-regulated learners. That may end up being more valuable than any piece of content you ever teach.

TEACHER TIP

ERIN BOUTILIER, HIGH SCHOOL SPECIAL EDUCATION TEACHER (ALEXANDRIA, VIRGINIA)

"I strive to set realistic expectations for my students that are achievable, but not too stringent that they get discouraged if they fall behind. It can be a challenging balance to uphold, but it is more important to ensure mastery at a manageable pace than to move on if there is no understanding of the content.

"Self-pacing also presents the opportunity for a tough life lesson that sometimes, you may have to cut your losses, do what you can, and move on. If at some point in future weeks a student feels like they are ahead, they can go back and finish something they may have skipped over initially."

Practice 5.2: Prioritize Your Content

Self-paced intervals help you balance the needs of your students with the demands of your curriculum. Within any given self-paced interval, however, you'll face another inevitable challenge: there's a lot you want to teach, and students like David can master content faster than can students like Anna or Troy. So you need a way to keep every learner, no matter how quickly they achieve mastery, appropriately challenged and supported—not just within each lesson, but throughout each self-paced interval too. How do you manage that?

First, if you commit to self-paced learning, you must accept the possibility that some learners may never master—or even reach—every piece of content you'd like them to learn.

This may be difficult to accept. If you care about your content, you surely want each of your students to master everything on your syllabus! But if you require that, then meeting every learner's needs becomes impossible: to have every learner cover the exact same content in the same amount of time, you'd need to give all your students the same lessons each day. In other words, you'd be back where you started.

In effect, you can either:

A. Push through all of your syllabus's content, with the understanding that some of your students may not master much (if any) of it.

B. Give your learners the time they need to master essential skills, with the understanding that they might not cover all of the syllabus's content.

As I think proficiency rates make clear, Option A—the traditional approach— doesn't work. When we present students like Anna and Troy with content they aren't prepared to understand, they only fall further behind, then feel less capable as a result. And when we stick too closely to one-size-fits-all syllabi, we deny advanced students like David the opportunity to excel.

If, however, you can move toward self-paced lessons, intervals, and courses, you can let David fly. You can help Anna master the essentials of your content, with the understanding that she can always catch up on the rest later. You can give students like Troy a fighting chance to succeed.

And from a learner's perspective, I believe that deeply understanding essential skills is preferable to only partially grasping a full year's worth of content. Deep understanding provides a foundation of knowledge from which students can build, along with the self-esteem that comes from mastering new skills. Pushing students through syllabus content that they aren't prepared to master—and therefore don't understand—accomplishes none of that.

The question then becomes: what content is truly essential?

I can't answer this question for you, as I don't teach your content. But I can share the framework I used, which today helps thousands of Modern Classroom educators prioritize their own content. I recommend you classify each task you give students as either:

◆ **Must-Do.** These activities cover skills and content which your students must absolutely master in order to succeed in your course. Students who don't complete these activities may develop significant learning gaps, which will prevent them from accessing more complex material later on. Therefore, completing these tasks—and more importantly mastering the underlying content—is non-negotiable.

◆ **Should-Do.** These tasks support student understanding, but can be skipped if students are short on time. Sometimes these activities cover content and skills that are interesting but not essential; in other cases, they provide practice or review that is helpful for students but not necessary. In other words, students can still understand the core content of your course without completing Should-Do tasks.

◆ **Aspire-to-Do.** These are the extensions that make your content most interesting—and fun! They should inspire students to apply their newfound skills in new and exciting ways. You can use these activities to motivate and challenge students like David, but it's also okay if learners like Anna and Troy don't reach them.

This can feel somewhat abstract, so I'll explain how it worked for me. In the trigonometry unit I described at the start of this chapter (Figure 5.1), I considered my lessons on the sine and cosine functions Must-Do: these are the most commonly used trigonometric functions, because they help humans model all sorts of interesting real-world phenomena, and it would be a shame to take precalculus without understanding them. My lesson on the tangent function, which helped students review and strengthen their knowledge of both functions and trigonometry, was useful but not as applicable, so I made it Should-Do. I also made my end-of-unit review lesson Should-Do: it was good for my students to review before the test, but not essential. And I found my lesson on inverse trigonometric functions quite interesting but not particularly useful, so it made a perfect Aspire-to-Do.

However you decide to prioritize your content, here are a few things to consider.

◆ **Classifying lessons vs. classifying tasks.** I usually found it simplest to label entire lessons as Must-Do, Should-Do, or Aspire-to-Do. Many Modern Classroom educators, however, label individual activities within each lesson, so that any given lesson has Must-Do, Should-Do, and Aspire-to-Do components. You can approach this either way! Classifying individual tasks is more complex to communicate, but offers greater flexibility.

◆ **Explaining classifications to students.** Most Modern Classroom educators explain the Must-Do/Should-Do/Aspire-to-Do framework to their students, then share each lesson or activity's classification. This clarifies the teacher's expectations and helps students understand what's truly essential to master.

If you do share these classifications, your students may ask whether they actually need to complete Should-Do and Aspire-to-Do work. I recommend that you tell them the truth—they do not—and also that you emphasize why completing these lessons or tasks will benefit them in the first place. Ideally, your students will see these assignments as challenges they feel excited and proud to tackle, rather than extra work they have to do.

And if you'd rather not share these classifications, you don't have to! If you have a strong internal sense of what content really matters, you can simply let students skip nonessential work—or give them extension activities—as the need arises. If a student falls behind, for instance, you might let them skip an activity you consider Should-Do; if a student gets ahead, you might have an Aspire-to-Do task ready to share.

Whether you share your classifications with students or not, your goal should be the same: to ensure that every student covers the essential content of your course, while offering students who are ready the opportunity to excel.

◆ **Number of classifications.** I liked having three different classifications, as it let me distinguish between activities that were useful but not essential (Should-Do) and activities that were true extensions (Aspire-to-Do). Some teachers, however, find it simpler to have only Must-Do and Aspire-to-Do activities, as two classifications are easier to manage and communicate than are three. As with every element of your Modern Classroom, you should do what makes most sense to you.

◆ **Grading implications.** Some Modern Classroom educators count Should-Do and/or Aspire-to-Do work as extra credit. Some give students grades up to a certain level (say, 80%) for completing Must-Do work, then grades up to higher levels (say, 90% and 100%) for completing Should-Do and Aspire-to-Do tasks. Some consider Should-Do and Aspire-to-Do activities valuable in themselves, and don't grade these tasks at all. And others take other approaches. As I wrote in Part 1, there isn't a right or wrong approach to grading in a Modern Classroom, but it's worth thinking through your approach in any case.

◆ **Terminology.** The terms Must-Do, Should-Do, and Aspire-to-Do work for Modern Classroom educators around the world, but there are lots of good alternatives too. I like "Need-to-Know/Good-to-Know/Aspire-to-Know," as well as "Proficient/Advanced/Expert." So long as you are clear, I encourage you to be creative!

Classifying your learning activities can be hard: if you care about your content, you'll be tempted to make most lessons or activities Must-Do. But remember: the more you require every learner to do, the harder it will be for you and your learners to prioritize. So commit to the essentials, and leave lots of room for learners to go above and beyond. That way, each of your students will be appropriately challenged—and therefore fully able to engage—every day.

RAQUEL GARCIA, K-5 SPECIAL EDUCATION TEACHER (CHICAGO, ILLINOIS)

"My 'Must-Do' tasks are essential activities that all students are required to complete as they align directly with grade-level standards. They represent the core content and skills that students must acquire to progress academically. 'Should-Do' tasks are activities or extensions that reinforce the strategy taught, and 'Aspire-Do' tasks include topics of personal interest, independent inquiries, or creative problem-solving designed to foster curiosity, autonomy, and self-directed learning.

"By categorizing tasks, I provide a structured framework that supports executive functioning skills like task prioritization, time management, and goal setting. This also allows for differentiation based on students' individual needs, interests, and abilities, ensuring that all learners have opportunities to succeed and thrive academically."

Takeaways: A Structure for Self-Pacing

Defining appropriate self-paced intervals and classifying content require challenging compromises between learners' needs and curriculum's demands. I often worried that by starting a new unit when some students hadn't fully mastered the last one, or labeling some of my content Should- or Aspire-to-Do, I was discouraging some of my students from mastering everything in my syllabus. This was never fully comfortable.

Yet it's important to remember that teaching traditionally—and pushing through content without giving learners the time they need to understand it—involves compromises too. When we present content to young people but move on before they master it, we make them feel inadequate and imply that understanding our content doesn't actually matter. So if we care about mastery, we must give students the time they need to achieve it.

Setting self-paced intervals and prioritizing content doesn't lower expectations for students—it raises them. It lets you hold your students to high standards of understanding on the content that really matters, and gives every student the opportunity to reach (and exceed) that level. And it sends the message that, if they invest the time and effort, every student is capable of true understanding.

MASTERY CHECK

Before advancing to the next chapter, please make sure you understand how to:

☐ Set appropriate intervals for self-paced learning.

☐ Prioritize content by classifying learning activities.

☐ Balance the needs of your learners with the demands of your curriculum.

These compromises make self-pacing possible. But once you've made them, you'll face other challenging questions. Within a given self-paced interval, for instance, how can you ensure that every student masters your Must-Do content? How can you make clear what each of your self-paced lessons actually entails? And if David does extension activities while Anna and Troy catch up, how do you keep them all on track?

If your students are going to learn as much as they can while progressing at their own paces, you need to make the learning process as straightforward as possible. And there's not a moment to waste.

Step 6

Develop Sustainable Systems

A single Modern Classroom lesson typically contains, at minimum, an instructional video, guided notes, collaborative practice activities, and a Mastery Check. Even a short self-paced interval can contain many times that—not to mention Should-Do and Aspire-to-Do activities that some students will attempt and others will not. That's a lot to keep organized.

You can't control the experiences, behaviors, or needs that your students bring to school—but you can control the systems that make your class run. Knowing where things are, and when and how they should be used, provides needed stability in a job whose day-to-day demands are often unpredictable.

As important as organization is for you, however, it's even more important for your students. Their time and attention is limited, and good systems direct as much of that time and attention as possible toward learning. The faster your students can figure out what they need to do, the more energy they can devote toward doing it.

Keeping students on task, of course, is a challenge in any classroom. It's often easier in a Modern Classroom—students are more likely to focus when they are appropriately challenged—but it requires that students know what they should be doing first. And without you lecturing from the front of the room, it's possible that some of your students will become distracted or get lost.

So if your students are going to navigate smoothly and independently from videos and guided notes to collaborative practice and individual Mastery Checks, they'll need clear guidance. They'll need to know where to find the resources they need, both digitally and on paper, and how to use each resource. They'll need to know where to access their work, where to submit it, and where to go when they need help. They'll need to know how to spend every minute of class, so they don't waste precious minutes wondering.

And you'll need systems for all of that.

CHAPTER OBJECTIVES

By the end of this chapter, you will be able to:

1. Organize digital content clearly in your learning management system.

2. Design your physical classroom to facilitate self-paced learning.

3. Create consistency and efficiency through well-planned routines.

If you want your students to reach mastery on their own, you'll need to show them the way. But learning can be challenging, and distractions abound. How, then, do you keep their path clear?

My Story: A Method to the Madness

My first self-paced interval was, frankly, a mess. My students understood what to do with each component of my lessons: they could watch a video and take notes, work together on practice, and take Mastery Checks independently. But in the transitions between these activities, they always seemed to get lost. I heard the same questions over and over. Where's the next video? How do I find the practice? Where do I turn in my Mastery Check?

Every time my students got stuck—and every time I had to redirect them— was time wasted. So when my students started to fall behind the suggested pace I'd outlined, I had myself to blame. I realized that I needed to get organized on three fronts.

First, I needed to clean up my learning management system (LMS): the online platform where I posted digital content for students to access. While all of my videos were linked there in a way that made sense to me, they weren't always easy for my students to find. I had to make my LMS as simple as possible for every learner to navigate.

Second, I needed to arrange my classroom in a way that facilitated the actions I wanted students to take. If I wanted students to go straight from watching my videos to completing practice on paper, I needed to make my practice tasks easy to find. If I wanted to give students feedback as promptly as possible, I needed a clear system for collecting and returning graded work. And if I wanted to stop running around my room answering questions, I needed a central place where students could come and get the help they needed.

Finally, I needed to define clear routines for key moments of class. When my students walked into my room, transitioned from our whole-class opening activity to self-paced work, and prepared to leave at the end of class, I didn't want any confusion about what students should do. If I wanted them to get right to work, I needed to be explicit about what that work entailed.

Like every Modern Classroom educator I've ever met, I needed time to develop and refine my systems. But once I found good ones, they made everyone's lives much simpler. If you're also ready to make teaching easier for you—and learning easier for your students—here's what you can do.

Practice 6.1: Simplify Your LMS

Digitizing digital instruction means putting a lot of content online. The natural place to organize it is in an LMS: an online platform where students can access digital content.

Your school or district likely provides an LMS, and if you can make that work, I recommend using it. Your students' other classes are probably there as well, so your students should already know how to log in, and there's likely someone in your school or district who can help you troubleshoot too. If you don't have a workable LMS, however, you can also just create a simple web page using a free tool like Google Sites.

As with video-recording software, the particular platform you use doesn't matter: it's how you use it that counts.[1] (In my own teaching career I used Blackboard, then Canvas, then Google Classroom, then Moodle.) You can organize any LMS in a way that is intuitive for students to navigate.

Whatever LMS you use, I recommend that you:

◆ **Start simple.** Many platforms come pre-loaded with a wide variety of features: announcements, discussion boards, etc. I recommend that you start by using as few of these

---

[1] Also as with video-recording software, I won't get too far into the details here: digital platforms change often, and different schools and districts use different platforms. If you're not sure how best to use your school's LMS, I encourage you to consult a tech expert in your school or district, or to visit www.meeteverylearners needs.org for detailed guidance on common LMS platforms.

features as possible: you want your students to get comfortable with the basic flow of your lessons before doing anything more complex. If you can, in fact, I recommend you hide or disable these unused features altogether. As your students become more comfortable navigating your LMS, you can experiment—but it's better to start with the basics.

◆ **Define a clear starting point.** Starting from the same place every day helps students get right to work. Whether it's the first page they see when they log in, or another page they need to open once they're in, make sure students know where you want them to start—and how to get there.

◆ **Use a consistent naming/numbering system.** If you have a lot of videos or other content to share, the easiest way to organize it all is by numbering each piece. Students will quickly understand, for instance, that Lesson 1.2 comes after Lesson 1.1, and this will help you order content logically on each page. You can also use consistent naming conventions to identify the different types of content—videos, readings, online practice, etc.—you choose to post.

◆ **Teach LMS use explicitly.** As with note-taking, you shouldn't expect that students will know how to navigate your LMS effectively—no matter how clear or intuitive it may seem to you. Consider printing out guidance or recording a video that explains to students how they should navigate your LMS, and posting that resource in a prominent place. This guidance makes your expectations clear, and can serve as a valuable resource for families and/or students who join your class mid-year.[2]

◆ **Learn from your students.** There's no better way to understand how your students experience your LMS than to watch them navigate it. You can do this intentionally—ask a student to find something and then sit with them as they try—or you can simply note the places where students always seem to get stuck.

---

[2] Before I adopted the Modern Classroom approach, receiving new students in the middle of the year was a nightmare: I somehow needed to orient them to my class while continuing to teach everyone else. Once I had videos and a well-organized LMS, however, it wasn't hard at all. I just told new students how to access the LMS and let them get right to learning.

This can be frustrating. I spent a lot of time making my LMS as simple as I thought it could possibly be, so I was often disappointed when my students struggled to navigate it. But they were doing their best, and the places they got stuck were ultimately places where I needed to be clearer—either in organizing my LMS or in explaining it to my learners. So I watched them navigate the platform, listened to their complaints, and did my best to improve my LMS in response.

Making your LMS easy to navigate is easier said than done. Once you've done it, however, self-paced learning becomes smooth, whether students are in class or at home. Learning an LMS also helps students become more comfortable using technology, which will serve them throughout their lives.[3]

So be open-minded and patient—and seek support from your school or district's tech experts when you need it. As you make continuous improvements, and your learners become more familiar with your LMS, you'll eventually arrive at a system that meets all of your needs.

TEACHER TIP

MOHSINA PATEL, PRINCIPAL (LUSAKA, ZAMBIA)

"I've seen an increase in my teachers' confidence due to the time and effort that we have taken to create instructional videos and an LMS that is clean, linear, and easy to follow. I can honestly say that our educators have a lot more confidence that we are doing literally everything in our power to make sure that our students are learning in the best possible way, and that has definitely increased our confidence as a whole school.

"In fact, we have had so much success with this model that we actually had two professors from universities in Zambia pay our school a visit, because they were so interested in finding out how we are teaching primary- and elementary-school students independent-learning skills that many university students lack!"

---

[3] Although today's students are considered "digital natives," they often struggle to use computers for productive purposes. So teaching them to navigate online is valuable in itself—and students agree. Compared to their peers in traditional settings, students in Modern Classrooms report that they are significantly more likely to learn how to use technology in class. See Morrison, J.R., Cook, M.A., Eisinger, J., & Ross, S.M. (2021). The Modern Classrooms Project: Evaluation Results for the 2020–21 School Year. Baltimore, MD: Johns Hopkins University.

Practice 6.2: Optimize Your Classroom Setup

What students do in your LMS matters, but accessing content online is only a small part of how they'll learn. Because students in Modern Classrooms spend most of their time working together off-screen, you'll want to be equally intentional about the way your physical classroom operates too.

As I wrote in Part 1, one way to do this is by designating classroom spaces for specific purposes, including peer collaboration, small-group instruction, and independent work. This creates clarity for students and helps you provide appropriate support as students tackle different kinds of tasks.

To help students move fluidly from task to task, I also recommend that you:

◆ **Make paper materials easy to gather and submit.** Students may access videos online, but they'll generally take guided notes and complete practice work on paper. If they can collect, store, and/or submit these papers on their own, they can go straight from one activity into the next without needing guidance from you.

To keep papers organized, you can use binders, folders, or stackable shelves, as well as turn-in bins near your desk. Label these clearly, and make sure students know how to use them. This helps learners progress independently, saves you time, and can be a nice way to get students up and moving during class too.

◆ **Consider where you'll spend your time.** Some Modern Classroom educators like to wander around their rooms asking and answering questions; others prefer to sit in one place and let students come to them. In my opinion, a mix of both strategies is ideal. Moving around helps you check in with all your students, while remaining in one place gives every student an equal chance to come and get your help. And while it's nice to circulate and sit down where students already are, there's a benefit to making students get up too: it's good for them to move around a bit, and it might also encourage them to save the trip by answering easy questions themselves.[4] There isn't one right place or way to spend your time, so find the setup that works best for you.

If your systems here are clear enough, your students should be able to complete entire lessons without ever asking you for directions. That means you can spend your time building relationships, fostering collaboration and discussion, and providing advice, feedback, and encouragement.

TEACHER TIP

AMY AZAROFF, MIDDLE SCHOOL SCIENCE & MATH TEACHER (COQUITLAM, CANADA)

"I have labeled boxes for notes, articles, practice, and any other paper materials that students might need, so students can access them independently. I also have basic school supplies and science materials like magnifying glasses and scales which they can use for activities.

"Mastery checks, on the other hand, stay with me. Once I see that students have completed their notes and practice activities, I give them the Mastery Checks directly. That way, I know they are ready—and if there's not enough time left in class, I can have them take the Mastery Check the next day. I also have a special turn-in box for Mastery Checks so that it's really easy for me to collect and assess them as quickly as I can."

Practice 6.3: Refine Your Routines

Once you've organized your classroom, students should know how to use each space of the room. Of course, they'll still need to know what to do, how to do it, and when. You can make that clear through effective routines.

---

[4] My students often got frustrated when they came to me for support and, rather than answering their questions directly, I sent them back to review my resources themselves. I admit this often led to slower resolutions in the short term! In the long term, however, students eventually learned to find answers on their own—and started paying closer attention to the resources I provided when they knew I wouldn't always just show them what to do. Teach a student to fish, in other words, and you feed them for a lifetime.

In any classroom, routines create consistency. Consistency, in turn, provides comfort: students know how to be successful without having to worry about what they are expected to do.

In a Modern Classroom, where students control their own learning, good routines are especially valuable. When your routines are clear, and your students understand them, you won't need to spend much time or effort giving directions: students will come in and get right to work, and you can spend your time supporting them. In fact, without the need for you to give directions or deliver direct instruction, your class will essentially start to run itself!

To reach this point, you'll need strong routines for:

◆ **Starting and/or ending class.** As I wrote in Part 1, most Modern Classroom educators like to start class with brief whole-class opening routines. These can include announcements, shout-outs, reviews of prior content, and/or fun activities that build community among learners. A consistent opening routine can take five minutes or less, and set learners up for a productive rest of class.

Some educators supplement these openings with a check-in form that gives students the chance to set goals, answer a warm-up question, and/or share how they feel that day (see Figure 6.1). Completing a brief form like this can help students determine what they want to achieve each day, while collecting students' responses can help teachers identify learners who may need additional support.

Name:	Today's date:	I am on lesson:
Today I am feeling: ☐sunny! ☐cloudy ☐rainy ☐stormy ☐other:_____		
My goal for today:		
Answers to warm-up questions:		
Anything else to share?		

FIGURE 6.1

A sample daily check-in form. The teacher collects this information, then uses it to decide who needs support. Some teachers use digital forms instead.

Many Modern Classroom educators incorporate similar closing routines as well. Setting aside a few minutes at the end of class can help learners reflect on their progress, identify next steps, and celebrate the achievements and contributions of their peers.

And while it's helpful to have consistent opening and/or closing routines, it's also okay to skip these when necessary. If your students just want to spend some days working at their own paces from bell to bell, it's nice to let them do that too!

◆ **Transitions to and from self-paced work.** If you do anything as a whole class, you need a way to move smoothly into student-led learning. You should tell students when and where they should access computers, how they'll know where in the room to sit, when they should move there, and where they should collect the materials they'll need. Once you've explained all this, challenge your students to make these transitions as quickly as possible—and let them know when they've done that well! Positive reinforcement always helps, especially when learners are doing something new.

And if you want your students to end class in a consistent way—performing a closing routine, for instance, or even just putting away materials—you'll want to plan and practice that transition too.

◆ **Collecting and reviewing Mastery Checks.** Some teachers like to leave Mastery Checks in a specific place in their classrooms, while others prefer to distribute Mastery Checks only on certain days, or when students request them. Any system can work, so long as students know how to collect Mastery Checks, where to work on them independently, and what to do with them when finished.

Because Mastery Checks determine what students should do next, you also need an efficient process for grading them and giving students feedback. Ideally, you can review students' work and return it, with written and/or oral comments, right away. Prompt feedback keeps learners on track and prevents learning gaps from forming.

But if you can't grade Mastery Checks right away—after all, you've got plenty of other things to do!—you should encourage students to start their next lessons while they wait: this prevents bottlenecks and keeps students engaged. Just make sure your students understand that, if you review their

Mastery Checks and identify misconceptions, they should go back to the previous lesson to revise and reassess before continuing with the next one.

At the very least, you should aim to grade Mastery Checks every day.

◆ **Answering student questions.** You will, as I've mentioned, get lots of questions. It's good to answer these questions promptly, so students don't get stuck—although making students wait a bit from time to time can also help them become more self-sufficient. You should also make sure you check in with students who don't always ask questions, so that those students who do ask more often don't monopolize your attention.

One good way to manage questions efficiently is by leveraging other students in your class: having students "Ask Three Before Me" or designating "teacher's assistants" to answer their peers' questions can save both you and your students time while fostering authentic collaboration. Another good method is to set up a "help desk," where you (and/or your teaching assistants) can sit during class, answering questions on a first-come, first-served basis. I've also seen some educators develop "question queues"— online or on a whiteboard—where students list their names when they have questions, and other educators give their students colored indicators (such as green, yellow, and red cups) that students can use to indicate when they need help.

Whatever system you choose, aim for consistency and predictability. When students know how to ask questions and how you'll respond, they'll feel comfortable requesting your assistance. They may become more discerning about what they ask, too.

Creating routines like these is a balancing act: you want consistency and efficiency, without sacrificing flexibility or overwhelming students with procedures. So your routines will evolve over time, as they should. What matters is that you think through each moment and potential challenge of class from the learner's perspective, and develop a clear vision for how your classroom will meet each learner's needs.

If you can do that, your Modern Classroom will eventually start to run itself. And you and your students can focus on what really matters: learning.

TEACHER TIP

LINDSEY ANDERSON, HIGH SCHOOL SOCIAL STUDIES TEACHER (SHENZHEN, CHINA)

"Each day, we start class by reviewing the pacing guide and discussing what is coming up in the unit. Then we often do a short whole-class activity or discussion that students can complete regardless of their progress. This helps students transition into class.

"Before moving to independent work, students review any feedback they have received and set a goal for the class. Students are asked to sit in groups with students who are at a similar pace. These groupings are projected as students enter class.

"Early in the year, I was very strict about expectations related to on-task behavior. I have found that this early consistency is crucial."

Takeaways: Organizing Chaos

To an outsider accustomed to teacher-led lessons, a Modern Classroom may look chaotic. There will be students all over your room, working on different things. You and your students, however, will recognize that every activity has its logical purpose and place. And your students should know, at all times, both what they are doing and why they are doing it. That way, they won't waste precious cognitive energy wondering whether they're in the right place.

So think about the spaces—both digital and physical—that will help your students work productively, as well as the routines and procedures that will keep your learners focused and engaged. Then bring those systems to life!

MASTERY CHECK

Before advancing to the next chapter, please make sure you understand how to:

☐ Organize digital content clearly in your learning management system.

☐ Design your physical classroom to facilitate self-paced learning.

☐ Create consistency and efficiency through well-planned routines.

In a Modern Classroom, however, keeping every learner appropriately challenged and supported requires more than just good organization. It requires every student to know, every day, what to work on next—in a classroom where twenty or more students may be spread across five or more lessons. You'll need a good system for that too.

Track and Communicate Progress

What makes Modern Classrooms responsive to learner needs is also what can make them challenging to manage: different students work on different lessons at the same time.

From a learning perspective, this makes perfect sense. Students need different amounts of time to master new content, which inevitably means they'll be in different places. David should work on Lesson 4 if he is ready for it, and Anna should not if she is not.

From a classroom management perspective, however, this can get complicated. You want each of your learners working on the right lesson—but how do you know who should be doing what? How does each student know what to do each day? And how should you decide where to spend your own time during class?

You can have engaging videos, clear Mastery Checks, and a well-organized LMS and classroom. But if you don't have a strong system for tracking what every student has learned—and communicating to each student what they should do next—it will be difficult for students to reap the benefits of self-paced learning.

Good progress trackers, in other words, are what make good Modern Classrooms run.

CHAPTER OBJECTIVES

By the end of this chapter, you will be able to:

1. Monitor each learner's progress through self-paced intervals.

2. Use progress trackers to motivate learners and foster collaboration.

3. Use data on progress to meet every learner's needs.

It can be hard enough, even when students are all working on the same lesson, to keep every learner on track. How do you manage it when every student is learning at their own pace?

My Story: A Sense of Where They Are

Mastery checks gave me precise data on my learners' progress: I knew at every moment what each of my students did and did not yet understand. I could, in theory, use this data to determine what each student should do next. In practice, however, I needed to organize it first.

So I created a simple chart (see Figure 7.1). Each row represented a student, and each column a Mastery Check. When a student completed a Mastery Check, I wrote an "x" in the corresponding cell; if the student instead needed to revise, I wrote an "r." I printed this chart and carried it around on a clipboard.

	Lesson 5.1	**Lesson 5.2**	**Lesson 5.3**
David	X	X	X
Anna	X	r	
Troy	X		

FIGURE 7.1
A snippet of the "clipboard chart" I used to track learner progress. Note that David had to revise his Lesson 3 Mastery Check; I updated his progress once he did.

This chart was simple to read and easy to update in real time. During class, it gave me a real-time snapshot of what my students understood—and therefore what each student should be learning next. I used the data from this table to plan my whole-class opening activities, pull small groups during class, and assign seating.[1] Plus, if a student ever forgot where they were in the unit or what they should do next, I could simply look at the chart and answer.

---

[1] I generally determined small groups and assigned seating based on progress, which was both efficient and equitable. In the past, I had generally grouped chosen groups and seating based on my own subjective (therefore biased) perceptions of students' aptitude or behavior. Now, when I wanted to assign seats and/or create groups of students to work together, I could use real-time data about their understanding to drive my decisions.

I soon realized, however, that my students were often forgetful. Once they got started, they knew what to do—but when they arrived the next day, many no longer remembered where they had left off. I ended up spending a lot of time reminding each student where to resume learning.

My students, it turned out, also needed a way to track their progress. So I created a simple checklist (Figure 7.2) and printed a copy for each learner.

These checklists, of course, would work only if students updated them. So I kept the checklists in my classroom—so students wouldn't lose them—and initialed them whenever students achieved mastery. Earning my initials on their checklists soon became a well-deserved badge of pride.

This system eliminated any start-of-class confusion—my students simply picked up their checklists and got right to work—but something was still missing. I was glad my students could easily follow their own paths, but I wanted them to work together too.

So to foster collaboration, I made one more chart, which I projected onto my board during class (see Figure 7.3). At the top of each column was the name of each lesson, and underneath it were the names of the students working on that lesson.

Unit 5: Trigonometric Functions

Lesson 5.1: Sine and Cosine Functions (Must-Do)
- ❏ Video
- ❏ Practice
- ❏ Mastery Check   Teacher Initials: _____

Lesson 5.2: Function Transformations (Must-Do)
- ❏ Video
- ❏ Practice
- ❏ Mastery Check   Teacher Initials: _____

Lesson 5.3: Sinusoidal Models (Must-Do)
- ❏ Video
- ❏ Practice
- ❏ Mastery Check   Teacher Initials: _____

FIGURE 7.2
Part of a checklist students used to track their progress through a self-paced interval. I initialed lessons once students completed those lessons' Mastery Checks.

This chart had two primary benefits. First, it helped learners confirm what they needed to do each day: the moment I displayed it, every student could get to work on the appropriate lesson.

Lesson 5.1: (Catching Up)	Lesson 5.2: (On Pace)	Lesson 5.3: (Ahead of Pace)
Troy Xavier	Anna (revise) Briana James	David

FIGURE 7.3

An example from my whole-class progress tracker, which I organized by lesson and used to encourage collaboration.

(If there was a discrepancy between a student's individual checklist and my whole-class chart, we could also address it right away.) Second, it made collaboration easy: students could look at the board to identify classmates to work with on a given lesson, as well as classmates who had already achieved mastery and whom they could therefore ask for help. My students no longer needed to wait for me to suggest partners or answer their questions. They could look at my tracker and take action themselves.

I was initially nervous about how this chart would be perceived, both by my students and by my community. I didn't want students to feel ashamed when they fell behind, nor did I want learning to become a competition. I also worried that parents or administrators might raise concerns about this chart's impacts on students' self-esteem.

To address these concerns, I presented this whole-class progress tracker in a deliberate way. This chart didn't reflect students' intelligence or potential—just the work they had invested to date. It wasn't a platform for competition—it was a tool to foster collaboration. And most importantly, it was never final. Every student could advance along the tracker if they put in the time and effort.

This system of tracking and communicating progress took me time and effort to develop and maintain. But once I and my students figured out how to use it, we saw several significant benefits:

◆ After my whole-class opening routine, every student could get right to work at the appropriate point in my self-paced interval.

◆ The satisfaction of progressing, on both their checklists and my whole-class tracker, motivated my students to achieve mastery.

◆ My students used my whole-class tracker to collaborate more effectively than ever before.

◆ I used data on progress to respond directly to each learner's needs.

It was ultimately my systems for tracking and communicating progress that made self-paced learning in my classroom smooth. And when I visit Modern Classrooms today, I often see educators using simple tracking systems to make self-paced learning efficient, collaborative, and fun. If you're ready to keep your own learners focused and on track, here's what you can do.

Practice 7.1: Monitor Each Learner's Progress

At any given moment, learners in your Modern Classroom will be doing several different things. This is good—it lets students reach mastery at their own paces—but it can easily become difficult to track.

To address this, you need a clear and efficient way to record what each learner has and has not yet mastered. Monitoring each learner's progress will help you determine what each learner should do each day—and therefore what support you can provide.

In my opinion, the easiest and most efficient way to monitor students' progress is by printing a simple chart to carry around during class. A clipboard chart like I used (see Figure 7.1) is easy to update—it takes just a few seconds to note when a student has demonstrated mastery or needs to revise—but provides precise data: the chart shows in one place what each learner understands, what each learner should do next, and how your class is progressing as a whole. Then, if you have an online gradebook that mirrors your printed chart, you can easily update progress on the computer at the end of each day.

Whatever system you use to record your learners' progress, I recommend that you:

◆ **Update it regularly.** Because it determines what each learner should be doing in class each day, your tracker is useful only if it reflects each learner's current understanding. Try to update it in real time if you can, and make sure to record all progress before your class meets again.

I realize this may seem cumbersome, especially if you already maintain a digital gradebook. But tracking progress in real time actually makes grading easier: you can grade students' work on the spot, note the grade on your chart, and enter it online after class. Then you can spend your planning time figuring out what to do tomorrow.

◆ **Look for trends and respond accordingly.** Your time in class is precious, and the data you collect on learner progress can help you figure out where to invest it.

If, for instance, your tracker indicates that many learners are stuck on a particular lesson, you can offer a small-group mini-lesson that gets them all unstuck. If you see learners getting ahead of your suggested pace, you can create more Aspire-to-Do activities, or recruit those learners as teacher's assistants. And if you notice that a particular learner has fallen behind, you can spend time with that student one-on-one, diagnosing the reasons they're behind and making a plan to get them back on track. This is data-driven instruction at its best: you're using real-time data on mastery to determine what to do in class every day.

You can also use your progress chart to help determine the right length for your self-paced intervals. If you start to see students getting further ahead or behind than you're comfortable with, you can reduce the length of time that students pace themselves between resets. If, on the other hand, you see students bunched together, you can give learners more autonomy by extending your intervals. It's okay—and natural!—for your students to be a few lessons apart, but you never want the gaps to feel insurmountable.

◆ **Use progress to foster collaboration.** When you know that two or more students are on the same lesson, you can encourage them to work together—or to ask classmates who have already mastered that lesson for help. Grouping students based on progress is also equitable: students' objective progress, rather than your or their subjective preferences, determines the groups.

If you like, you can also assign seating based on progress. I liked doing this for two reasons. First, it helped students who might not otherwise interact get to know one another: if they were on the same lesson, they could sit at the same table and form a relationship by working together. Second, it made my life easier! If a student had a question about a lesson, they could ask their tablemates; if multiple students had the same question, I could visit their table and help them all at once. Group work at these tables wasn't forced: it was an authentic way for students to learn from each other.

With Mastery Checks and a progress chart, you no longer have to speculate about what students understand or need—it's right in front of your eyes. And you can use this data to support every learner, every day.[2]

TEACHER TIP

LAURA DOMINGO, MIDDLE SCHOOL ELA TEACHER (GREENSBURG, INDIANA)

"I used to be intimidated by data, but now I have the confidence to embrace it. Because my students have become such strong independent learners and I can pinpoint more accurately their challenges, the data I collect from Mastery Checks give us all a clear picture of where we need to dig in deeper. My progress tracker reflects where everyone is and helps me determine if I need to work with students who are falling behind.

"My students are really learning because of the targeted support I can provide and the opportunities they have to review and reassess. As a result we are moving through the curriculum faster and with better results."

Practice 7.2: Give Every Learner a Map

It's important for you to know what each student should be learning at any given moment. It's even more important, however, for each student to know that! So if you want your classroom to run efficiently, you also need a clear way of showing every learner what they should do next.

At first, self-paced learning can be disorienting for students. They can no longer just come in, sit down, and do the same thing as everyone else. Instead, each learner must enter your classroom and figure out what to do each day, as well as where and how to do it.

---

[2] Compared to their peers in traditional classrooms, teachers in Modern Classrooms are significantly more likely to understand what each of their students has and has not mastered, and to use data to provide effective targeted support to students. See Wolf, B., Eisinger, J., & Ross, S. (2020). The Modern Classrooms Project: Survey Results for the 2019–20 School Year. Baltimore, MD: Johns Hopkins University.

In my experience, giving young people this kind of autonomy and ownership helps them build valuable executive-functioning skills like goal setting and time management. Yet these skills emerge over time, and require support to develop. Too much flexibility, without clear structure or guidance, can increase students' cognitive load and leave them feeling overwhelmed.

Every day, therefore—either when they enter your room or after your opening routine—every student should receive clear guidance on what exactly they should do next. (Some students will remember from the previous class, but others will not.) Once they know what to do, they can get right to work.

The easiest way to provide this guidance is to give each learner a "map" to the lessons in your current self-paced interval. This can be as simple as the checklist I used (see Figure 7.2), or it can be more creative: I've seen some Modern Classroom educators create actual maps, or "game boards" (Figure 7.4), that make learning feel fun.

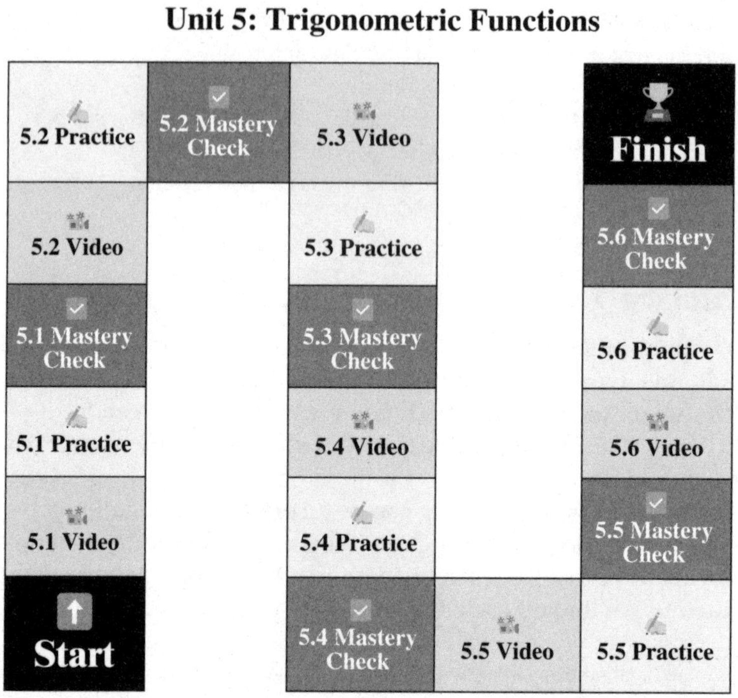

Unit 5: Trigonometric Functions

FIGURE 7.4
A sample game board for an entire self-paced interval. I used the simple checklist in Figure 7.2 instead, but I've seen many Modern Classroom educators use game boards like this one with great success.

However you create them, your progress maps should:

◆ **Outline clearly what each self-paced interval contains.** Your learners should see, in one clear place, everything they need to do within the current self-paced interval. This helps them set goals and understand where they are relative to the suggested due dates you've set.

Communicating clearly here is also a good exercise for you, as it forces you to plan a logical path through your content in advance. Even if you're still recording videos or tweaking Mastery Checks during the interval, creating a map ahead of time helps ensure that each of your self-paced intervals is fully and thoughtfully planned.

◆ **Let students indicate their own progress.** When a student completes an activity or masters a lesson, they should record their accomplishment! Checking a box or earning a sticker may seem like a small reward, but it provides positive reinforcement and helps learners stay on track. Once a student has marked off Lesson 1, for instance, they'll know to get started on Lesson 2 next.

And when it comes to Mastery Checks, many Modern Classroom educators like to sign or stamp their students' maps. This is easy to do if your Mastery Checks are on paper: you can simply sign or stamp each student's map when you return their work. This makes Mastery Checks feel special, and ensures that learners don't mistakenly skip over lessons that they have not yet mastered.

◆ **Be easy for you to check.** Progress maps are great because they give learners ownership—but there's always a risk that students will mark the wrong boxes and get lost. To prevent this, I recommend that you periodically check students' maps against your own progress tracker. Checking learners' maps keeps learners on track and creates accountability: if students know you'll be verifying their progress, they'll be more conscientious about marking it correctly.

This doesn't need to be a formal or time-consuming process: you can simply check students' maps throughout class, as you circulate your room to check in with learners. Or, if students leave their progress maps in class with you—which also prevents students from losing them—you can do a brief spot-check after class. Over time, students will understand that they need to track their progress accurately, and they'll get better at it too.

Creating progress maps for your learners facilitates good planning on your part, then helps every learner identify exactly what to do next. Once your students know how to read these maps, they can get straight to self-paced work every day, with minimal direction from you.

TEACHER TIP

JESSICA BILLE, K-5 SPECIAL EDUCATION TEACHER (LYNN, MASSACHUSETTS)

"The progress tracker is a natural motivator for my students. They like to see their names move from lesson to lesson. A student who is falling behind can get a lot of motivation by advancing on the tracker after each step they have taken!

"As a result, my students challenge themselves every day to stay on track. They are using time more wisely, taking control of their own learning and setting goals for themselves to keep up with their friends. Self-pacing teaches them responsibility and holds them accountable. And my students LOVE the independence and opportunities for collaboration which this model provides."

Practice 7.3: Encourage Collaboration With a Whole-Class Tracker

Progress maps help learners stay on track, but they risk making learning a solitary pursuit. If every learner is following their own individual path, when will learners come together to tackle common challenges—and learn from each other in the process?

As I explained in Part 1, strong collaboration is essential to a successful Modern Classroom. When students work together, they don't just build teamwork and communication skills: they also solve problems faster and save you work! Plus, learning with classmates is usually more fun than learning on your own.

In my experience, one of the best ways to foster collaboration in a self-paced environment is to display each learner's progress on a single tracker, which all learners can see. The table I used to organize learners by lesson, for instance, didn't just show students where they were in my unit—it also showed students which classmates they could work with and ask for support (see Figure 7.3).

Displaying a tracker with every learner's progress has other advantages too. First, it's efficient: every student can look at the same source to determine what to do next. If your students have progress maps, they can use your whole-class tracker to verify that their maps are up to date; if you choose to assign seating, students can use the tracker to figure out where to sit. These charts also let you recognize progress publicly: when a student advances, both you and their peers can celebrate their hard work! Finally, you can use the board where you display progress to display announcements and other resources. Your students will check their progress on the tracker, so they'll read anything else you post there too.

If you do choose to use a whole-class progress tracker, you should present it to your students carefully: this is a tool to encourage collaboration and effort, not cause competition or shame. And for these trackers to work, you must keep them updated, on at least a daily basis. (Some teachers like to update their trackers during class, which students often find motivating.) While updating student progress regularly is a good practice in any system, it's particularly important when your whole-class tracker helps students determine what to do next.

If you do use a whole-class tracker to foster collaboration, I encourage you to:

◆ **Explain its purpose to students—and other adults.** Presenting your tracker as a tool to provide clarity and foster collaboration is essential. I've found that, once students understand why their progress is displayed in this way, they rarely seem to mind. (This included my own students, as well as students I've met in Modern Classrooms around the country.) In fact they find it useful, and take great pride—as they should!—in seeing their names advance as a result of their hard work.

It's also important to frame the tracker in this way to colleagues, administrators, or parents, who may be concerned about how the public display of progress will be perceived. In fact, these adults will often be more skeptical of this approach than will your students themselves! You should explain it to them in the same deliberate way you present it to students.

◆ **Allow for anonymity.** If you or your students prefer not to use names on the tracker, you can use student-chosen nicknames, emoji, or student ID numbers instead. This makes collaboration somewhat harder to foster—the value of using names is that students know whom they can ask for help—but it preserves the efficiency of a single tracker that shows every learner's progress.

◆ **Consider letting students update it themselves.** If you have an interactive whiteboard or physical system for tracking progress—I've seen educators indicate learner progress with magnets, clothespins, velcro stickers, and more—you can further empower students by letting them update their progress themselves. This is fun for students, and another nice opportunity for learners to get up and move around the classroom.

If you do let students update their own progress, just make sure to check—ideally after each class—that they have done so accurately. You should be able to reconcile your own internal progress tracker, like my clipboard chart or your online gradebook, with whatever you display publicly.

For teachers who choose to use one, a whole-class progress tracker becomes a Modern Classroom's dashboard: it's the chart that shows each student what to do each day, and it informs the teacher's choices of where and how to spend their time. It's also an indicator of a well-run classroom, as implementing an effective whole-class tracker requires both strong systems and a classroom culture that supports collaboration. When I walk into a Modern Classroom and see an updated tracker on the board, I know immediately that it's a place where all students can truly learn.

TEACHER TIP

JOSEY ALLEN, HIGH SCHOOL SCIENCE TEACHER (LOVELL, WYOMING)

"My whole-class progress tracker has been highly motivating to students. Most students take it as a personal challenge to be on pace daily and a source of pride to be 'Rockin' It' (ahead of pace). For those who have been consistently off pace, I have individual conversations with them, starting with things outside of school then working towards their pace and learning progress.

The relationships I have developed from these conversations have, in almost all cases, had really positive effects. These students are now mastering many more learning objectives because they can go at their own paces and achieve a standard of mastery, instead of just moving on to the next lesson because that's what everybody is doing on that day. And the tracker gives me the data I need to pinpoint and efficiently close learning gaps."

Takeaways: Giving Students Ownership

It may seem difficult to keep every student in a Modern Classroom on track. In fact, I think it's much easier than in traditional classrooms: self-paced learning ensures that students are appropriately challenged, which naturally motivates them to engage. All young people, after all, want to succeed! You just need systems that show them how.

So once you have these systems in place, your class will start to function like a well-oiled machine. Your students will know what they need to do next, and feel responsible for accomplishing it. And you'll have the data to give your students the help they actually need.

Tracking and communicating progress, in other words, brings the potential of a Modern Classroom—every student appropriately challenged and supported, every day—to life.

MASTERY CHECK

Before advancing to the next chapter, please make sure you understand how to:

☐ Track each learner's progress through self-paced intervals.

☐ Use progress trackers to motivate learners and foster collaboration.

☐ Use data on progress to meet every learner's needs.

Systems like these, however, will work only if your students are willing to follow them. To truly meet your learners' needs, therefore, you'll need *their* hard work and commitment too. That's where motivation becomes essential.

Inspire Students to Excel

Every student wants to learn, and every student is capable of learning anything.

But learning is hard, and learners are easily distracted—or, worse, discouraged. If school isn't appropriately challenging, or if students don't feel appropriately supported, they will disengage. Their intrinsic motivation for learning will wane. And extrinsic motivation has its limits when students don't see school as a place where they can succeed.

So we teachers do our best to hold learners' attention. We use various classroom-management techniques—praise, warnings, grades, calls home, elaborate systems of consequences and rewards—to control students' behavior, in hopes that compliant students will be able to learn. Yet there's only so much any teacher can do to engage a student who already knows the content, or who is not prepared to understand it. And the more time the teacher spends managing behavior, the worse the underlying problem—the fact that students aren't appropriately challenged in the first place—becomes.

Modern Classrooms allow for a different approach. Rather than controlling student behavior in order to deliver content, Modern Classroom educators use appropriately challenging content, and appropriate supports, to encourage productive behavior. When students are engaged in learning, in other words, they'll behave. There's no better way to manage a classroom than by providing instruction that meets every learner's needs.[1]

---

[1] In one study, every Modern Classroom educator surveyed agreed that they could effectively manage student behavior, compared to only 78% of their traditional peers. Students in Modern Classrooms were also more likely to report that they behave well during class. See Wolf, B., Eisinger, J., & Ross, S. (2020). The Modern Classrooms Project: Survey Results for the 2019–20 School Year. Baltimore, MD: Johns Hopkins University.

But Modern Classrooms do more than just keep learners engaged. In fact, Modern Classrooms allow for learning experiences that truly inspire students. When teachers have the time to get to know—and thereby motivate—each of their students as human beings, and when those students can build self-esteem by developing real mastery, there's no limit to what young people can achieve.

Once you've inspired your learners, in fact, everything else becomes easy.

CHAPTER OBJECTIVES

By the end of this chapter, you will be able to:

1. Build strong personal relationships with each of your learners.

2. Use incentives to push all learners toward mastery.

3. Foster social–emotional growth through consistent reflection.

A Modern Classroom creates the conditions for every learner to excel. But how do you convince each learner that they actually can?

My Story: Engagement as Behavior Management

In my first few months at Eastern, I spent a lot of time policing students' behavior. I asked David to stop chatting with his friends, told Anna to take her head off her desk, and required Troy to enter my room silently if he arrived late. Not only was this exhausting—for me and for my students—but it meant I had less time to teach my content. I ended up getting frustrated a lot. Why, I wondered, didn't my students just pay attention?

Eventually, I realized the answer: they didn't see much value in it. David already knew what I was going to say; Anna couldn't understand it, and Troy, when he arrived, was usually lost. Once I understood this, it was hard to blame any of them. My students weren't struggling to learn because they were distracted. They got distracted because they weren't learning.

Adopting the Modern Classroom model, therefore, didn't just help each of my students learn. It also made class much less stressful—for all of us! When David, Anna, and Troy were appropriately challenged and supported, they rarely caused problems. And when they did lose focus, it was easy for me to address behavior challenges one-on-one, without disrupting the rest of my class. As the year went on, I spent less and less time managing behavior, and more and more time supporting learning.

Still, there were challenges. (There always are!) While some students took the autonomy my classroom provided and excelled right away, others struggled with their newfound freedom. Students like David didn't always see the value of pushing themselves, while students like Anna and Troy often doubted their own ability to catch up if they fell behind. Without the strict and familiar structure of a traditional lesson to drag them along, some of these students risked disengaging even further. I still had students act out, and from time to time I still saw heads down on desks.

Yet I knew that my Modern Classroom would meet these learners' needs more effectively than traditional lessons could—and I saw an opportunity to address the root causes of their disengagement. I now had the time to sit down with each of these young people, to learn who they were and what they cared about, and to connect their goals and interests with my own. I had the freedom to address students' conflicts and concerns one-on-one, in a compassionate and supportive way. (No more behavior showdowns in front of the whole class.) I had the chance to teach them more than just precalculus, and I leapt at it.

So I thought about the habits, mindsets, and social–emotional skills I wanted my students to develop, then gave them explicit opportunities to grow in those ways. I didn't just tell them to work harder: I showed them, through Mastery Checks and my progress trackers, that their hard work would pay off. I didn't just expect that they would learn from their mistakes: I pushed them to reflect on their successes and areas of improvement. And I didn't just assume that they would turn into resourceful, resilient learners on their own. I sat down with them and helped them become the scholars—and people—I knew they could be. We supported one another, and we all learned more too.

Students' apparent lack of motivation is probably the most common challenge that Modern Classroom educators—and maybe all educators—face. But deep down every young person wants to succeed, and Modern Classrooms create conditions where every learner truly can. Once students realize that, they'll be more motivated to learn than ever before.

If you're ready to inspire your learners, here's what you can do.

Practice 8.1: Embrace the Challenge

When you're standing at the board delivering a traditional lesson, you can get away with assuming that your students are following along. When you put students in control of their own learning, however, you can no longer assume anything: your data on mastery tells you exactly what students do and do not yet understand. And if you haven't yet figured out how to motivate every learner, you may realize that some students actually aren't learning much at all.

Many beginning Modern Classroom educators, in fact, have the same disheartening experience. They work hard to plan courses that meet every learner's needs, and most students engage—but some may not. These learners can fall behind. And these educators, who want *all* their students to succeed, aren't sure how to respond. This happened to me, and it might happen to you.

If it does, don't worry: this is perfectly natural. Learning is hard, young people are easily distracted, and your approach is new. It will take some students longer than others to adjust. (The first time I was given the freedom to learn at my own pace, I floundered a bit, too.) And your data on progress will help you identify those students who need extra support and encouragement before they fall too far behind.

So what may seem like a challenge is actually an opportunity. Your students can't hide anymore: you'll know whether they are learning or not, and you can take action right away to support the students who aren't. Remember that every young person wants to learn, and that success breeds success: once a student achieves their first taste of mastery, they'll be both eager and prepared to keep learning more. And the less motivated a student initially appears to be, the greater your opportunity to show them that they really can succeed—and the larger the impact you can make on their life.

So take heart! In creating lessons that every student can master at their own pace, you've created the opportunity for all of your learners to succeed. Now you just need to help them seize it.

Teacher Tip

Aviva Stern, Middle School English Teacher (Efrat, Israel)

"I see an incredible opportunity to teach work and life skills through self-pacing. Students are so used to being told what to do, and simultaneously they are kids with a natural tendency to push boundaries. In self-paced classes, where there is more freedom and less to rebel against, they are able to thrive, and they are also challenged by the opportunity.

"At first, my students struggled with their newfound independence. They had lots of questions and needed time to adjust to new systems. But that's part of the process! Some students experienced frustration, but even dealing with that frustration is a valuable skill in work and life. Our focus is now on the actual learning process, and my students have figured out the behaviors that help them succeed."

Practice 8.2: Invest in Relationships

Every teacher wants students who are intrinsically motivated. If students come to class wanting to learn, our jobs become easy! The question is: how do we make students excited to learn?

To me, the answer starts with relationships.

Intrinsic motivation, by definition, comes from students themselves. Motivating students intrinsically, therefore, requires you to learn who your students really are—and to care about who they'll become. Remember, students won't care how much you know until they know how much you care.

Fortunately, Modern Classrooms give you ample opportunity to show that. When you can sit down with your students, you can discover what matters to them, and what they want to achieve. Once you understand your students as people with their own hopes, interests, and dreams, you'll understand how to get the best out of them. And once they know you value them as human beings, your students will want to make you proud.

As with any relationship, developing close bonds with your learners requires both effort and intention. You need to spend meaningful time with each of your learners, and you must truly want to form meaningful relationships. If those two things are true, then I recommend that you:

◆ **Dedicate time to personal conversations.** Every learner in your class is a unique human being—and the best way to get to know them is simply to talk with each of them one-on-one. The sooner you can do this, the better.

So once your students are comfortable learning on their own, make a concerted effort to meet with every student individually. You don't need to talk for long—even a few minutes can be significant—and you don't need to discuss school. Instead, take these conversations as precious opportunities to learn what each student cares about, what they like doing, and what inspires them. Not only will you have information you can use to motivate each student, but your students will know you are genuinely interested in them as people.

And there's no reason to do this just once! The more often you can have conversations like this, the closer you and your students will become.

◆ **Develop a check-in routine.** When you're no longer delivering live direct instruction, you'll have the time every day to see how each of your learners is doing. This may sound like a lot, but it can be as simple as walking around your room during class and greeting each of your learners. A brief but sincere "how are you?" can go a long way.

If you'd like to approach this in a slightly more formal way, you can also create a system for your check-ins. As part of your whole-class opening and/or closing routines, for instance, you can use a brief goal-setting form (see Figure 6.1) to ask students how they feel, then collect their responses and decide whom you'd like to speak with further. A process like this allows students to share how they are feeling in a confidential way, and helps you figure out who most needs your support.

◆ **Celebrate every learner.** In a Modern Classroom, every student can reach mastery. Therefore, every student can accomplish something worth celebrating! Whether it's completing an Aspire-to-Do activity or mastering a challenging lesson after three attempts, acknowledging these accomplishments is always meaningful—especially for students who aren't used to being recognized in an academic setting.

These celebrations don't need to be fancy. You might share shout-outs at the start or end of class, or display on your whiteboard the names of learners who have recently excelled. However you share this recognition, make sure to monitor whom you praise when, so you can be sure to celebrate every learner at some point.

And once you have this system in place, consider sharing these celebrations with other adults in your learners' lives! A quick email to a student's parent, guardian, or coach can mean a great deal—especially when it's backed by real evidence of that student's growth.

Once your learners realize that you know who they are, understand that you care about each of them, and see that you will recognize their hard work, they'll be eager to do their best.[2]

ZACH DIAMOND, MIDDLE SCHOOL MUSIC TEACHER (WASHINGTON, DISTRICT OF COLUMBIA)

"I get to be authentically myself in the classroom. I used to have to put on a persona—my 'teacher voice'—but I never really felt like that was me. Now that I don't have to lecture to my students, I don't have to ask a big group of kids to sit quietly and compliantly while I talk to them, so I don't have to control their behavior so much anymore. Instead, I get to be myself, and I get to chat with the kids.

"So we talk about music in a way that feels authentic to me, and it helps me to build much stronger relationships with all of my students because I spend time talking with them. I'm not pretending to be somebody who needs to control them in order for them to be successful. And my students feel like they can be themselves too, because we are not trying to fit into this classroom mold that some of us don't feel comfortable in.

"What it boils down to for me is the feeling of being in a classroom with a bunch of human beings that I can relate to. That is the biggest change in my classroom now that I'm implementing Modern Classrooms, and I'm not ever looking to go back."[3]

---

[2] Compared to their peers in traditional classrooms, students in Modern Classrooms are significantly more likely to agree that they have good personal relationships with their teachers, that their teachers provide personal support and encouragement, and that their teachers care about them as individuals. See Morrison, J.R., Cook, M.A., Eisinger, J., & Ross, S.M. (2021). The Modern Classrooms Project: Evaluation Results for the 2020–21 School Year. Baltimore, MD: Johns Hopkins University.

[3] Zach created and—as of this writing—still runs the Modern Classrooms Project Podcast (podcast.modernclassrooms.org), which regularly features Modern Classroom educators discussing their practice. It's a great listen! You can also read more about Zach's approach to relationship building in "Students before Content: The True Power of Relationships in the Classroom." Next Generation Learning Challenges, January 6, 2020.

Practice 8.3: Use Incentives Strategically

I truly believe that strong relationships can motivate young people to achieve anything they set their minds to. But if we want our students to push themselves, supplementing those relationships with a few extrinsic incentives can't hurt.

I have always been skeptical of systems that rely on rewards and consequences to motivate learners. I worry that they obscure the innate joy of learning, and have found them difficult to implement equitably. Every learner is unique, so an incentive structure that is fair in theory may impact different students differently.

With that said, I think incentives have value too. When used effectively, incentives make your criteria for success explicit, then reward students for achieving those criteria. I was certainly motivated by rewards and consequences throughout my academic career, and I imagine your students can be too.

So while you continue to build relationships with your students, I encourage you to institute a simple and clear system of incentives, all designed with the end goal of mastery in mind. In my experience, the most effective Modern Classrooms combine human connection with appealing incentives so that it's clear how students' effort is rewarded—and so every student is excited to work hard as a result.

Incentives that work well in Modern Classrooms include:

◆ **Progress-based perks.** Achieving mastery is inherently rewarding, but it's nice to be recognized too. Many Modern Classroom educators provide students who are ahead of their suggested pace with special privileges, such as choice seating or free time during class. Others award more traditional incentives—stickers, snacks, etc.—based on progress. Just make sure that the criteria for earning these rewards are clear, and that all students have the opportunity to earn them.

◆ **Teacher's assistant roles.** Once learners have mastered a lesson—and if they are willing—they can help their peers! I've seen educators nominate "Lesson Superstars" or give students "Genius Badges" for the day, so their classmates know where they can go for help. Not only does this recognition reward students for showing mastery, but it can also foster peer collaboration and save you work.

If you do this, try to include as many students as possible as assistants throughout the school year, and remember that becoming a teacher's assistant can be a powerful motivator for students who need to catch up.

◆ **Soft zeros and/or extra credit.** There's no right way to grade in a Modern Classroom: it depends on your personal philosophy as well as your school's policies. However, if you do give grades regularly, there are two techniques I've seen educators use to motivate their students.

The first is what I call the "soft zero": entering a zero grade as a placeholder for required work that a student has not yet mastered. While this will temporarily lower that student's grade, it sends a powerful message about the importance of Must-Do work, and gives the student a clear incentive to reach mastery. Seeing the zero replaced with a mastery score also provides an immediate reward for the student's hard work. If you do institute this policy, I recommend that you explain it clearly to your students, administrators, and families—and that you award students full credit as soon as they complete missing work.[4]

The second strategy is providing some kind of extra credit for Should-Do and Aspire-to-Do activities, or requiring students to complete these activities to reach certain grades. (For instance, you can require Should-Do work for grades above 80%, and Aspire-to-Do work for grades above 90%.) You shouldn't need to do this—these extension activities should be valuable both in themselves and as preparation for culminating assessments—but I've seen many educators use this approach effectively. After all, it never hurts to reward students for going above and beyond. And who doesn't love a little bit of extra credit?

Whatever incentives you provide, be sure to explain their rationale and award them in an equitable way. Fortunately, offering

---

[4] If it were up to me, all students in a given class would start the year with a gradebook full of zeros and work their way up from there. By the end of the first quarter, their goal would be a grade of 25%; by the end of the second quarter they'd aim for 50%, and so on. This would, however, be a significant departure from the conventional approach to grading, in which students start at or near 100% (based on the first grade they receive) and generally drop from there. So when I used the "soft zero," I entered zero grades only once the suggested due dates for each of my lessons had passed.

incentives based on demonstrated progress—as opposed to more subjective factors such as behavior—is inherently fair: if the criteria for mastery are clear, then every student should have the same opportunity to reach them. And your targeted support can help ensure that every student does.

Ultimately, the motivational strategies that work in a Modern Classroom—relationships and incentives—work in traditional classrooms too. But the flexibility which Modern Classrooms create, for both teachers and students, enhances your ability to invest in both strategies. You'll have the time to build close relationships, and your students will have the time to earn mastery-based rewards. That way, all of you can succeed.

TEACHER TIP

KHADEJAH SCOTT ARTIS, MIDDLE SCHOOL READING SPECIALIST (WASHINGTON, DISTRICT OF COLUMBIA)

"One way I motivate learners is by inputting 'Waiting for Submission' in my gradebook for students who have not completed a self-paced task by the due date. After the student completes the missing task, I will update their grade.

"Another system that is helpful for motivating learners is our weekly raffle. As students follow expectations, they earn raffle tickets and positive narration. Once a week, I randomly pick two to three students to get a prize.

"As a result, I've noticed that my students' perseverance has increased, and students are always willing to revise until they get it right—even practice assignments! Seeing 'revise' on the progress tracker is not a cause for embarrassment; it's an opportunity to earn 'mastered' on the second try after some practice. Since they see a clear path to mastery as they complete the tasks in a module, my students are more invested in their learning than I've seen before."

Practice 8.4: Foster Growth Through Reflection

Our young people need to master academic content and skills. What students learn in school helps them understand their worlds, and the skills they develop will prepare them for meaningful lives and careers. Mastering new things also builds young people's confidence and self-esteem.

I believe, however, that it's equally if not more important for our students to develop as learners and as human beings. In other words, school should help young people become better at the process of learning itself, and more aware of their personal strengths and opportunities for growth. This will set learners up for success no matter where their lives lead.

In a Modern Classroom, you can foster learners' social–emotional development through consistent reflection. Students should consider, at regular intervals, questions that help them grow: What am I doing well? Where can I improve? What helps me succeed? What gets in the way? And what do I need to accomplish my goals? These are simple questions, but what students learn by answering them can be profound.

Fortunately, because students in a Modern Classroom are responsible for their own learning, they'll have plenty of learning experiences—both good and bad—to reflect upon. To make this reflection as effective as possible, I recommend you:

◆ **Create a simple reflection form.** If you want your students to focus on the substance of their reflections, make the form in which they reflect as clear as possible. I've found that simple, open-ended questions often elicit the most meaningful responses. A basic reflection form (see Figure 8.1) should take students no longer than five minutes to complete.

   These questions should also help students look forward as well as back: while reflection forces students to look at the past, it's ultimately meaningful because it helps learners adjust their behavior in the future.

◆ **Collect students' responses.** Reflection is valuable in itself, but it will be most useful if you take the time to read—and respond to—what students have written. This will also motivate students to take reflection more seriously.

   If you have students reflect on paper, consider marking each student's reflection briefly—not to award a grade, but to highlight areas where you agree. If you have students reflect on a digital form instead, consider maintaining a record of each student's reflections over time. (This can be very helpful at parent–teacher conferences!) Whichever method you choose, remember that quick one-on-one conversations about the content of students' reflections can be productive too.

Name:	Today's date:
What did you do well this week?	
What will you do differently next week?	
What feedback do you have for me?	
Anything else to share?	

FIGURE 8.1

A sample weekly reflection form. You can also use an online form, which makes ongoing data collection easy.

◆ **Make reflection a regular practice.** Reflection is most valuable when consistent: like anything, your students will get better at it with practice. And if you ask the same questions each time, your students can start to think ahead about how they will answer—then adjust their behavior accordingly.

In terms of timing, I recommend giving your students some kind of reflection at the end of each self-paced interval. This is a natural moment for learners to identify where they have succeeded and struggled, and a good time to consider how they'll do better during the next interval. You can always have students reflect more or less frequently too.

Finally, be sure to tell your students why they are spending valuable class time reflecting. Once students understand how reflection benefits them, they'll welcome the opportunity to grow.

There's a lot going on in your Modern Classroom. But if you can remember to ask your students the same simple questions on a regular basis—then take the time to read and respond to what they write—both you and your students will start to notice patterns.

You'll recognize where each learner needs to improve, so you can start to push them in those directions. Your learners, meanwhile, will start to notice the behaviors that do and do not help them succeed, then start to self-correct without assistance from you. And if you can collect students' responses over time, you'll have a way to show students—and the adults in their lives—just how far they have come.

A good Modern Classroom helps students develop knowledge and skills. A great Modern Classroom helps them develop as people too.

TEACHER TIP

LYDIA CRUSH, HIGH SCHOOL ELL TEACHER (CHESTERFIELD, VIRGINIA)

"My students complete a Daily Do Now where they review their progress tracker, set a daily goal, and think about how they are feeling that day. Talking with students about their goals helps them see that 'Learn English' might not be an achievable goal in one class period, but that 'Complete Lesson 5.3' could be.

"I use an end-of-unit reflection to help students be more aware of what habits are helping them be successful and which aren't. I also ask them what parts of the unit they would like me to keep and which I should not use again. It's helpful for me to know what my students want more of and what my students dislike.

"Reflection helps my students feel supported and seen, so they are more willing to take risks and try things that are difficult for them. Because of this, I'm also seeing academic progress in students who would otherwise get lost in the system."

Takeaways: Your Real Impact

Our greatest opportunity as educators is the chance to shape the people our students become. So once you've planned lessons that meet every student's needs, and woven those lessons into cohesive self-paced courses, you can get to the most impactful, most important, and most interesting work there is: helping young people grow, not just as learners but also as human beings.

MASTERY CHECK

You've almost finished Part 2 of this book! Before advancing to the next chapter, please make sure you understand how to:

☐ Build strong personal relationships with each of your learners.

☐ Use incentives to push all learners toward mastery.

☐ Foster social–emotional growth through consistent reflection.

I believe that a single Modern Classroom can transform a young person's life. The experience of working hard to achieve mastery can show learners like David and Anna and Troy—perhaps for the first time in their academic careers—that if they apply themselves to appropriately challenging content, they can truly succeed. And when learners see themselves as capable of success, they are.

Yet students' identities as learners develop over many years, in many courses, through thousands of individual lessons. If those courses meet learners' needs, our young people will form positive attitudes toward learning—and toward themselves in the process. But every course that fails to challenge or support young people diminishes the value they place on learning, and threatens their self-esteem in the process. It's no wonder, after all, that Anna felt like she couldn't understand math. That's what years of traditional instruction had really taught her.

So if we want every young person to flourish throughout their educational careers—and throughout the lives that follow—we need as many courses as possible to meet every learner's needs. One Modern Classroom is a start, in other words, but it's not enough. From their first day of kindergarten to their last graduation ceremony, every young person deserves learning experiences that provide an appropriate level of challenge and support. Every young person, in every classroom, deserves instruction that unlocks their full potential.

And you can help make that happen.

Part 3

Redesigning Instruction

I was one teacher with a good idea.

Then Kareem visited my classroom and launched his own Modern Classroom. Now there were two of us.

Then our colleagues noticed. Then their colleagues. Then teachers across the district, the country, the world. They adopted our approach as well. Now we are thousands.

Yet millions more teachers are struggling. Millions more students are languishing. And millions of families, administrators, and policymakers are wondering how best to meet their students' and teachers' needs.

So your opportunity here is enormous. And it isn't just to plan better lessons or teach better courses.

You have the chance to transform instruction itself.

The Challenge of Instruction

Put enough lessons together and you'll get a course. Put enough courses together and you'll get school: the system through which our young people receive close to 15,000 hours of instruction by the time they turn 18.[1]

Unfortunately, much of this instruction fails to meet our learners' needs. Remember that, in 2022:

◆ Only 36% of American fourth-graders were considered proficient in math, and just 33% were considered proficient in reading.[2]

◆ By eighth grade, only 26% of American eighth-graders were considered proficient in math, and just 31% were considered proficient in reading.[3]

◆ Only 22% of American high-school graduates were considered ready for college.[4]

Proficiency rates have barely budged over the past thirty years, and it's not hard to see why: the traditional method of one-size-fits-all,

[1] This estimate comes from the National Center for Education Statistics's Schools and Staffing Survey. Chronically absent students like Troy receive many fewer hours, but they still spend a staggering amount of time in school. See "Average number of hours in the school day and average number of days in the school year for public schools, by state: 2007–08." *National Center for Education Statistics*, https://nces.ed .gov/surveys/sass/tables/sass0708_035_s1s.asp.
[2] See National Assessment of Educational Progress. 2023. "NAEP Report Cards." http://nationsreportcard.gov.
[3] Ibid.
[4] This is the percentage of students who met all four college-readiness benchmarks on the ACT test. See "Grad Class Database 2022—ACT Research." 2024. ACT. http://www.act.org/content/act/en/research/services-and-resources/data-and-visualization/grad-class-database-2022.html.

one-lesson-per-day instruction hasn't changed either! Despite massive investments in testing, curriculum, and educational technology, the average classroom today doesn't function all that differently than it did a century ago. The same old models of instruction produce the same lackluster results.[5]

We continue to invest our most precious resource—our young people's potential—in our schools, and the vast majority of those young people fail to master the skills we say they need. By the time they turn ten years old, two out of three Americans are already considered below proficient in reading—and most just fall further behind as they continue through school. We can, and must, do better.

And while proficiency rates can feel abstract, there's a real human cost here. Young people like David spend years of their lives in math classes that fail to challenge them. Young people like Anna, meanwhile, spend years feeling overwhelmed, and young people like Troy spend years feeling lost. These students are wasting time they can't get back! And if we don't appropriately challenge or support them now, we set them up to fail later on.

As I hope I've shown, none of this is your or your students' fault. Your students come to school wanting to learn, and you show up every day wanting to teach. The problem is that traditional, one-size-fits-all lessons and courses simply don't meet anyone's needs.

Modern Classrooms can. They help young people achieve mastery and teachers feel successful. And they can empower teachers and students in any school, any grade level, and any subject area, anywhere in the world.

So if you agree that this approach better serves teachers, students, and the world, you may aspire to lead change beyond your classroom walls. You may wonder: how do I get my community invested in this style of teaching and learning? How can I share what I'm doing with colleagues who might benefit? And how can I shape the larger conversation around what education should be?

---

[5] Shane Donovan, who taught high school science using a self-paced, mastery-based approach before I even became a teacher, makes this point using a metaphor I like. In Shane's words, "No matter how good you are at trying to do one-lesson-per-day, all-kids-together, teacher-led instruction, it's just a fundamentally flawed model that was designed for an Industrial Revolution time and workforce, and it hasn't been updated in 150 years. Making improvements within the traditional paradigm is sort of like training a decent horse to be an incredible one, when in fact there is a car available. The mechanics and design of a car just give it a massive advantage."

To answer these questions, you'll first need to articulate—to yourself and to others—exactly why our current system is so inadequate. Our young people's futures, after all, depend on you. And only once you truly comprehend the problem can you offer its solution.

CHAPTER OBJECTIVES

By the end of this chapter, you will be able to:

1. Articulate the challenges posed by age-based education.

2. Empathize with students who are unable to succeed in our existing school system.

3. Define the characteristics of instruction that meets every learner's needs.

If we want all students to succeed, we need to prepare them properly—from the day they enter school to the day they leave. Here's why our current system sets them up to fail.

My Opportunity

The end of my first year at Eastern should have been a time for celebration. My students and I had grown close, and by May I think we genuinely enjoyed learning math together. As graduation drew nearer, however, I started losing sleep. No matter what I tried, there was a question I couldn't escape.

Were David, Anna, and Troy really prepared for what would come next?

Don't get me wrong: I was proud of what I had been able to teach, and of what each of my students had been able to learn. David had prepared himself for calculus, Anna had mastered composite and trigonometric functions, and Troy told me that he had learned more math in my class than in the rest of high school combined. These were real accomplishments.

But when I stepped back and considered the skills and mindsets that each student would ultimately take from their larger K-12 experiences, I felt angry. David may have been the best math student at Eastern, but he could have learned more elsewhere. Anna may have mastered my Must-Do lessons, but there remained significant gaps in her mathematical understanding, not to mention the lingering emotional scars of her previous math failures. Troy had learned when he came to class, but he had missed huge amounts of content, both in my class and in others. I knew how much potential each of these young people possessed, and I didn't feel that any of them had come all that close to realizing it.

My precalculus class had been a good one, but it came too late. By the time they reached me, my students had experienced many years of math instruction that had failed to meet their needs. Their skills had stagnated, and their attitudes—toward math, toward school, and toward themselves—had suffered too. In the ten months we had together, there was only so much I could do to overcome the skill and self-esteem deficits they had accumulated over the past ten years.

When I shared this with my colleagues, I realized that they all felt the same way—no matter what grade levels or subjects they taught. We all faced classes full of learners who were ahead, behind, or chronically absent. We all struggled to cover everything in our syllabi. We all tried to do the very best we could. But none of us ever felt it was enough. So we felt inadequate too.

There was an opportunity here: not just to help my colleagues redesign their lessons or their courses, but also to reshape our students' entire educational experience, at Eastern and beyond. If we as a community could redesign instruction to meet every learner's needs, from their first day of school to their last, we could help David, Anna, Troy, and all of their classmates achieve their true potential. They could all reach my precalculus class and be prepared to excel.

First I had to understand why they weren't.

Pass and Fail

The gaps between learners start at birth. Young people's lives and futures are shaped by who their parents are, where they grow up, and countless other environmental factors beyond their control.

In theory, school should give all young people an equal opportunity to succeed. Yet in practice, school often serves only to widen the gaps between learners. And if you consider individual students' experiences, you can see why.

Think about David, Anna, and Troy as fifth-graders. David, like approximately one-third of ten-year-olds nationwide, was proficient in fourth-grade math, so he understood everything in fifth grade too. Anna, however, had missed important concepts in fourth grade, so she missed even more in fifth grade. (It's impossible to construct advanced knowledge on an incomplete foundation.) Troy, who was often absent, likely understood even less. So at the end of fifth grade, David again proved proficient, while Anna was again considered below proficient. Troy missed the test altogether.

The next fall, however, we put these students back in the same sixth-grade class! They were a year older, after all. And in sixth grade, the same thing happened: David excelled, while Anna and Troy fell further behind. It happened again the next year, and the year after that, and so on. So by the time they reached me, David could understand composite functions almost immediately, while Anna still wasn't sure what x represented in an equation. The gaps that started at birth had grown tremendously.

In a world in which we expect all students to graduate high school by the age of eighteen, it's not hard to see why we let this happen: we don't see other good options. Holding students back carries a stigma, and it's not clear that having Anna or Troy repeat fifth grade would do them any good in the first place: Anna's learning gaps go back further than that, and Troy is absent half the time anyway. We could put David into an advanced class and Anna and Troy into a remedial one, but this also seems unfair: putting Anna and Troy onto a slower-moving track now, when they are only ten years old, may mean that they'll remain in remedial classes for the rest of their academic careers. And while we could ask Anna and Troy to attend summer school or after-school tutoring, there's no guarantee these interventions will make much difference either—or that either student will even be able to attend. These options all feel like punishment, but neither Anna nor Troy has done anything wrong.

So we pass them along and hope that, next year, they will somehow be able to catch up on what they missed, while learning the next year's content at the same time. This rarely happens. But what else can we do?

Within any given course, the Modern Classroom model can help. In my classroom, for instance, Anna and Troy really could learn the fundamentals of precalculus. But they came to me so far behind, and with so many gaps to fill, that they had little real hope of reaching Should-Do or Aspire-to-Do content. My classroom met their immediate learning needs. Yet by no fault of their own, they still missed out.

As I hope this example shows, passing students along to content for which they aren't adequately prepared ultimately sets those students up to fail. We teach them along the way that understanding content doesn't actually matter, and we let many of them graduate without the essential skills they need for college and career.

Worst of all, however, we shape the way they see education in the first place—and, therefore, the way they see themselves.

How Instruction Feels

By the time they reach precalculus, my students have spent significant portions of their lives in school. Starting in kindergarten—if not before—they have received some form of instruction for roughly seven hours per day, 180 days per year, for twelve long years.

That's a lot of time. It's also a precious opportunity. What students take from their K-12 education, in terms of both knowledge and mindsets, will in many ways shape how they spend the next sixty-odd years.

So in addition to the content they do (or don't) learn, it's worth considering what our students really take from their experiences in school. After years of traditional instruction, in other words, how do David, Anna, and Troy feel about learning in general? And how do they see themselves?

◆ **Students like David, who are proficient or advanced, feel overly confident.** After excelling for years in math classes taught to the middle, David feels invincible. He has rarely encountered a problem he can't easily solve.

Yet math is hard, and no one is invincible—especially as math becomes more complex. And when I do give David an Aspire-to-Do problem he can't easily solve, I often see him give up. David hasn't often felt challenged in school, so he hasn't yet learned how to persevere through tough problems. Nor, for that matter, does he know how to get help, either from his classmates or from me. In classes that haven't challenged him, he has never really needed to.

David has the talent, motivation, and self-confidence to become the engineer he aspires to become. But to succeed in college and beyond, he'll need humility, problem-solving skills, and the ability to collaborate productively with his classmates. I know that my Modern Classroom can give him those things! But we've got a lot of work to do.

◆ **Students like Anna, who are far behind, feel inadequate.**
Anna believes she is bad at math, and it's hard to blame her:
she has now spent many years suffering through math
classes she hasn't been prepared to understand. She has
failed her year-end standardized tests year after year, and it
never seems to matter. She gets passed along with her
classmates and set up to fail again.

In the short term, advancing Anna from one grade to the
next may seem like it's in her best interests. It saves her the
stigma of being held back and keeps her off the remedial
track. Yet doing this year after year imposes real psychologi-
cal harm: Anna loses confidence in her very ability to succeed.
That's why she puts her head on her desk: she knows she
isn't prepared for precalculus, so why bother? She'd rather
just rest. And pretending not to care feels much safer than
trying to listen, failing to understand, and feeling inadequate
all over again. Anna feels insecure about her ability, and
apathy is her defense mechanism.

Anna, like every young person, is capable of succeeding in
math. But she has to believe in herself first. Unfortunately,
very little in her educational experience to date has helped
her do that.

◆ **Students like Troy, who are chronically absent, feel
ignored.** I don't know about you, but I always dreaded
coming back to school after missing class. I hated feeling lost,
and I worried that I'd slow my class down or embarrass
myself if I had a question about something my classmates
already understood.

I imagine this is how Troy feels every time he comes back
to school. I imagine it's miserable.

There are things Troy's teachers can do to help him catch
up. They can give him packets of makeup work to complete,
or make him copies of their notes. But Troy needs more than
just the sheets of paper he missed—and his teachers have
limited time outside of class to help him. It's too easy for
Troy to get lost in the shuffle.

So Troy comes to class when he can, despite the challenges
he faces. He dutifully collects his makeup work packets and
notes. But he realizes in the process that his teachers can't
really provide the support he needs. So in some way it's a
wonder that he continues to come back at all.

Depressing as this all is, it's hard to fault my former students for their attitudes—and pointless to blame them. The way they approach school is ultimately a function of the learning experiences we have given them. And if we want them to like learning—and to love themselves—we need to rethink the way those experiences feel, from the day they walk into school to the day they walk across the stage.

Toward Better Instruction

It's easy to criticize the system that exists and hard to propose a better one. Our school system is complex. Changing the way our students are educated would be a massive undertaking.

But our current system isn't working—at least not for students like David, Anna, or Troy. And if we want to improve it, we must consider what kind of instruction, from kindergarten through high school and beyond, would actually meet David's, Anna's, and Troy's diverse needs.

In an instructional system that truly helps every student succeed:

◆ **David would always feel challenged.** As soon as he learns something new, David should advance to the next lesson— with no limit to how far or how fast he can go. And if David masters a course's content early, he should move directly to whatever comes next, whether that's meaningful extension activities or another course altogether. No longer bored, David can soar.

◆ **Anna would always feel supported.** Anna should never be rushed through content she isn't yet prepared to understand. Instead, she should have the time she needs to master each successive skill, alongside teachers and classmates who can answer her questions and encourage her when she struggles. It's true that Anna might not get quite as far as David. But with the right support she can actually understand everything she encounters, and develop the foundational knowledge to continue advancing even after school ends.

◆ **Troy would always feel capable of success.** We want Troy to come to school every day, but we know that may not be possible. So we should give Troy the next best thing: the opportunity to master content whenever he can, and the ability to pick up each day wherever he left off the last time. When he comes to school, therefore, he can be just as engaged and successful as every other learner. He'll feel motivated to learn when he's in class, and may be inspired to catch up outside of class too.

In a system like this, each of these learners—and their teachers—could make efficient use of class time, then continue learning freely on their own once class ends. Each of these learners could achieve mastery without feeling bored, lost, rushed, held back, or confused; their teachers could provide the support each learner needs without becoming frustrated or overwhelmed. Everyone in every classroom, in other words, could truly succeed.

MASTERY CHECK

Before advancing to the next chapter, please make sure you can:

☐ Articulate the challenges posed by age-based education.

☐ Empathize with students who are unable to succeed in our existing school system.

☐ Define the characteristics of instruction that meets every learner's needs.

An entire school system like the one I've just described may sound impossible to create. I don't think it is. It begins with you.

Prepare for Launch

You now understand both how Modern Classrooms work and why they are necessary. What should you do next?

If you want to meet every learner's needs, it's time to start implementing what you've learned. I realize how daunting that can seem! This approach may be different from the way you currently teach, the way you were trained to teach, and the way you were taught as a student. It may not match the kind of instruction your students, their families, or your administrators expect. And it may sound like an awful lot of work. Trust me: I and every other Modern Classroom educator have experienced those same doubts. I know from experience how intimidating this all can feel.

But trust me on this too: there are simple steps you can take, today, to get started. I took these steps myself at Eastern. Every teacher quoted in this book has taken them, alongside thousands of their peers. And if they can launch their own Modern Classrooms in all different grade levels and content areas, all around the world, then you can too.

CHAPTER OBJECTIVES

By the end of this chapter, you will be able to:

◆ Explain how and when you will launch your Modern Classroom.

◆ Set students up for success with an effective self-paced orientation.

◆ Make teaching in a Modern Classroom sustainable.

The need is there. The solutions are here. What are you waiting for?

My Story: A Fresh Start

My Modern Classroom evolved gradually throughout my first year at Eastern. I began by using instructional videos, then incorporated collaborative practice, started sitting down with my students, and replaced simultaneous Exit Tickets with just-in-time Mastery Checks. From there I developed and refined my systems for prioritizing content, organizing my LMS and classroom, tracking and communicating progress, and inspiring each of my learners to excel. By June, my class looked nothing like it had in September.

Fortunately, my students were receptive to these changes. Maybe it's because they had seen how ineffective my traditional lessons were, or maybe the gradual pace at which I introduced Modern Classroom practices gave them the opportunity to adapt over time. They realized I was making continual improvements to better meet their needs, and they were generally happy to follow my lead.

So by the end of that school year, I was comfortable with the systems I had built—and excited to implement them right away in the fall. But I also knew that in August I would get a whole new set of students. And these students wouldn't experience a gradual adjustment process: I planned to start with a full Modern Classroom on the first day of school. I wanted each of these new students to understand, from day one onward, both what I was doing and why.

I decided to spend the first few days of school explaining how my Modern Classroom would work. And because I realized that some students would get the idea quickly, others would take longer to understand, and others would miss the first week of school altogether, I decided to explain my approach in a way that I knew would meet all these learners' needs: with a self-paced orientation that my students could master before we started learning math.

I called this orientation "Unit Zero." I took the slides I had previously shown on the first few days of class—explaining who I was, what I expected, and what my class would cover—and recorded short videos instead. I created icebreaker activities that students could complete collaboratively, Mastery Checks about my expectations, and a simple progress tracker. I made this brief unit the only thing visible in my LMS, then printed clear instructions for my students to log in. And when my students arrived on that first day, I greeted them, introduced myself briefly, then announced, "It's time to learn! Grab a computer and get to work."

This approach had several immediate benefits:

◆ **It made my expectations clear.** Right away, my students understood that they would control their own learning, and that I would be there for support. My Unit Zero also showed students that my instruction would be different from the traditional teaching they had come to expect.

◆ **It gave students an early experience of success.** My Unit Zero videos, practice activities, and Mastery Checks were about me and my approach, not my content. Every student, therefore, could easily achieve mastery, regardless of their prior math knowledge. In mastering Unit Zero, they proved to me—and more importantly to themselves—that they really could succeed in a self-paced learning environment.

◆ **It let me start building relationships right away.** In my first year at Eastern, I spent most of my first week standing in the front of the room, speaking to all of my students at once. This helped them get to know me, but didn't help me meet them.

But now, while my students engaged independently in my Unit Zero, I could walk around my classroom and introduce myself to every learner in a way that felt personal. By the end of my first week, I'd held at least one meaningful conversation with every one of my students, and I was well on the way to building relationships with each of them.

There were also benefits beyond that first week. When students joined my class midway through the school year, it was easy to orient them: I just started them on Unit Zero. When parents or guardians asked me how they could best support their students, I sent them my introductory videos. And when administrators visited my classroom, either informally or for evaluations, it was easy for me to explain my methods. I had already done that in Unit Zero.

That doesn't mean my first full year of implementation (my second year at Eastern) was always smooth. As in the previous year, there were times when I fell behind in planning, or lost my patience, or tried new systems that didn't work. But I recognized that these challenges were part of the learning process. I did my best to reflect, to be patient with myself, and to remember that I was growing too. That helped. And so that year, and every year that followed, I continued to tinker. While my lessons were never perfect, I always knew that I was doing the best I could to meet every learner's needs.

If you're ready to put everything you've now learned into practice, here's what you can do.

Practice 9.1: Start Small

A fully functioning Modern Classroom takes time and commitment to build. But as I hope my story has shown, all it takes to get started is a series of small action steps. If you can follow the guidance in Parts 1 and 2 to create Modern Classroom lessons and courses, you'll be most of the way there.

Then, once you have your lessons and systems planned, you just need to decide when you'll launch them—and which students you'll launch them with. As you make those decisions, I encourage you to:

- **Start with a single prep.** If you teach multiple subjects, grade levels, or courses, choose one to "Modernize" first. This keeps your planning load manageable, and lets you refine your approach before rolling it out more broadly.

  If you're not sure which subject, grade, or course to choose, I recommend you start with the content you feel most comfortable teaching. This will help you focus on the delivery of that content, rather than the content itself, and maximize the chances that your first Modern Classroom lessons will succeed.

- **Launch at the start of your next unit.** It's nice to launch your Modern Classroom at the start of the school year, especially if you've learned this approach over the summer, but it's certainly not necessary! In fact, starting in the middle of the year has advantages too: you already know your students, so you can tailor your lessons and systems accordingly. And the sooner you launch, the sooner you'll be able to start learning and improving.

  If you do launch mid-year, I recommend leading your first few Modern Classroom lessons at the start of a new unit. This is a natural transition point for both you and your students.

- **Plan a few lessons in advance.** Even a single Modern Classroom lesson can be a transformative experience, for you and your students alike. But you'll really see the power of this approach if you can start with a three-lesson sequence. That will give students like David the chance to move ahead quickly, students like Anna the time they need to achieve mastery, and students like Troy the chance to start at the beginning, whenever they arrive. It will also give you some breathing room: if you've planned a few lessons ahead, you can focus on facilitation without worrying about what fast-moving students will do next.

With that said, I would advise you not to prepare too many lessons before you launch. It may sound appealing to have several units' worth of content planned ahead of time, but it's better to have the flexibility to adjust your lessons once you see how your learners respond. So once you have three consecutive lessons planned, I'd say you are ready to go.

As with anything new, your first few Modern Classroom lessons will be the hardest to plan and implement. But they also provide the greatest opportunity for you to learn! You'll see right away what works, as well as what can be improved.

And while I hope these first lessons will inspire you to keep implementing and improving, you certainly don't have to! If you give this approach an honest try and don't think it will work for you or your students, you can always go back to what you were doing before. Trying a new approach for a few lessons won't hurt, while testing new techniques—and learning about yourself and your students in the process—can only help.

You may not like teaching in a Modern Classroom. Or, like thousands of educators worldwide, you may want to teach this way for the rest of your career. The best way to discover that is to start small.

TEACHER TIP

LINDSAY ARMBRUSTER, MIDDLE SCHOOL HEALTH & PHYSICAL EDUCATION TEACHER (BURNT HILLS, NEW YORK)

"I started by giving my students self-paced work. My students thrived, so I started exploring the model more. The next fall I started creating my own videos, and that winter I added in Mastery Checks. What started as a way to teach health education turned into a way to teach students to be learners and productive humans with a side of health education—and that is so much more important and impactful for adolescents.

"Initially I used this model with just eighth-grade classes and planned on continuing to teach my sixth-grade classes in a more traditional way. However, once I started with the model in eighth grade, I witnessed and experienced so many benefits that I just couldn't go back to traditional teaching. I now use this approach with all of my classes, including the two graduate courses I teach at a local university.

"My approach to my Modern Classroom has gone through many iterations, but one thing that has stayed the same—I have always been and will always be revising and refining, just like my students."

Practice 9.2: Prepare Students With a Self-Paced Orientation

Ultimately, what determines the success of your launch isn't how well you plan: it's how well your students respond. The better your students understand how your class works—and how they can succeed in it—the more likely it is that they will flourish.

So when you first launch your Modern Classroom, you'll need to explain clearly how your class operates. And while you can certainly explain the Modern Classroom model from the front of your room, I've found it more effective to introduce students with a brief, self-paced orientation. That way, students can learn your approach by following it!

Creating a self-paced orientation has other benefits too. For students, it can provide an immediate taste of success and serve as a reference throughout the year. For families and administrators, it's a nice way to get to know you and your approach. And for you, the exercise of creating a strong orientation helps you get really clear about both how your classroom will work and how you expect learners to succeed. Once you know that and feel comfortable communicating it, you'll be ready to go. Plus, you can re-use this orientation every time you get new students, whether that's at the start of a new school year or when students join your class mid-year.

I recommend that this orientation include a few short lessons—each with its own video, collaborative practice activity, and Mastery Check. Those lessons should:

1. **Introduce you.** The first thing you would do in a traditional classroom is introduce yourself, so it's how you should start your self-paced orientation too. (Of course, it's good to offer a live introduction first!) It's also nice if this first lesson tells students what they can expect from the orientation itself.

For collaborative practice here, you can ask students to introduce themselves to one another—this is a great opportunity for icebreakers and community-building. And for a Mastery Check, you can make sure your students know a few basic things about you. If these facts are easy to gather from your introduction, every student will experience early success.

(Note that if you are launching your Modern Classroom mid-year, you can skip this lesson. You may, however, end up creating it later for the students you get next year.)

2. **Describe how your class will work.** Next, explain your systems and procedures. Your students need to know how they will access and submit work, track their own progress, demonstrate mastery, and revise and reassess when necessary. This explanation makes the general principles of your Modern Classroom concrete.

Then let students learn by doing! If you explained how students will access and submit work, ask them to find a practice task and turn it in. If you explained how learners will track progress, give out progress maps and have your students mark them up. And if you explained the process of mastery assessment, let students experience it with another simple Mastery Check. You can use the content of these tasks to reinforce your systems and routines as well.

3. **Tell your students how to excel.** The actions students must take to succeed in Modern Classrooms may be different from what was required in traditional classrooms. So be explicit here: what kind of behavior do you expect from students, and how can they exceed those expectations? As on Mastery Checks, being clear about the criteria for success makes that success more likely.

Ideally, the collaborative practice that follows your explanation can start to instill these habits. Consider, for instance, having students submit their notes for review, or asking them to reflect on their strengths and weaknesses when it comes to time management. And for the Mastery Check, make sure students really understand what success in your classroom requires. Once they do, they'll be prepared to achieve it.

Throughout this orientation, you can continue to build community through whole-class opening and/or closing routines, as well as collaborative small-group activities. Helping students feel comfortable with one another is as important as making them familiar with your systems and routines.

By the time your students complete your orientation, they won't need to be told how self-paced learning works. They will have experienced it—and succeeded—themselves!

And while it's nice to give your students this kind of orientation at the start of the school year, when you might otherwise spend class time explaining procedures and expectations, a self-paced orientation can be equally helpful when launching your Modern Classroom mid-year. In that case, investing a day or two to reset and clarify your expectations will make everything that follows smoother. Plus, you can reuse these lessons as a "Unit Zero" at the start of next year too.

Once your students have mastered your self-paced orientation, they'll be prepared to succeed on everything that comes next.[1]

TEACHER TIP

CAROL MADRUGA, MIDDLE SCHOOL MATH TEACHER (KAPA'A, HAWAII)

"I launched at the beginning of the school year with a Unit Zero to explain how my classroom would work. I explained to my students that this was new, and we would be working through some issues together as I figured out how my teaching style meshed with Modern Classrooms. They appreciated this honesty, and their feedback during the implementation process helped me meet their needs."

"Since implementation, I have been able to build relationships with my students on a deeper level more quickly, because I have more time to spend getting to know my students. I can work one-on-one with students or in small groups, which allows me to have conversations with them about so many topics. I can better support them in their math understanding, but I can also understand what they have going on in their lives. Class time is more flexible now."

---

[1] It's good to put Unit Zero in your LMS so that your students can get used to the LMS. Once you've done this, you can also put the same materials on a publicly accessible Google Site, which is easy to share with parents, colleagues, and administrators. You can find a customizable Google Site template for Unit Zero at www .meeteverylearnersneeds.org.

Practice 9.3: Keep Your Workload Manageable

Once you've chosen a launch date, planned your first few lessons, and prepared a self-paced orientation, you'll be ready to meet every learner's needs. Before you do, though, there's something you must remember. Your Modern Classroom will work for your students only if it works for you too.

As educators, we often find it hard to prioritize our own needs. We become teachers because we want what's best for young people, and as a result we often struggle to set boundaries between our work and our lives. If you believe that a Modern Classroom will be best for your students, and commit to investing the time and energy that planning Modern Classroom lessons and courses can entail, you may find those boundaries even harder to maintain.

I don't want to dissuade you from working hard—and I'm confident that this approach will save you time and effort in the long run. But I believe that you'll be both happier and more effective if you can find ways to make planning for your Modern Classroom sustainable. Here are a few ways to do that:

◆ **Leverage existing resources.** Over time, you'll develop videos and practice and Mastery Checks that are tailored to your learners' needs. But that takes time, so as you're getting started I encourage you to lean on materials that already exist. If your school provides a curriculum, for instance, you can use that curriculum's activities and assessment questions as practice and Mastery Checks.[2] If not, you can usually find good materials online. And if you haven't had time to record a particular video yet, or don't plan to record videos at all, don't worry! You can find great explanations online too.

◆ **Alternate between intervals of Modern and traditional instruction.** I believe that you and your students will love Modern Classroom instruction. But I know that creating new Modern Classroom lessons takes time—and I may also be wrong about what you and your students will actually prefer.

---

[2] For more guidance on implementing a Modern Classroom with a school-provided curriculum, visit www.meeteverylearnersneeds.org.

One way to both test my hypothesis and make planning more manageable, especially in your first year of implementation, is to teach one self-paced interval, followed by one teacher-led interval. If you do this—and if you don't mind the traditional instruction too much—then you buy yourself time: you only need to "Modernize" half your lessons the first time around. You'll also understand which approach really works best.

◆ **Embrace change, within reason.** When you've worked hard to develop and implement a new system, it can be challenging to make adjustments. You may feel embarrassed to admit that something isn't working, or you may worry about confusing your students with yet another new process. Iterating on everything all the time can be exhausting, and you need time to rest and reflect too.

Sticking with systems that aren't working, however, can make both you and your students miserable. I recommend, therefore, that if you identify changes you want to make, you implement those changes at the start of your next self-paced interval. This provides consistency within each interval, while giving you plenty of opportunities to make improvements over time.

So when your next interval does start, don't be afraid to change things up! If you think an adjustment will improve your and your students' experiences, you're probably right. And if you're wrong, you'll learn. As you iterate, you'll surely improve.

◆ **Teach one day at a time.** You might occasionally feel like you should have more lessons planned, or that your students should be further along in your self-paced intervals. That's natural. But when class starts, there's no use in worrying about it! You've planned what you've planned, your students are where they are, and it's your job to meet their needs with whatever you have ready. If you can do that today, you can do it tomorrow too. And every lesson that helps students achieve mastery is an accomplishment worth celebrating! In the daily grind of the school year, it's worth pausing to appreciate that.

◆ **Give yourself grace.** Your Modern Classroom will never be perfect. In your first year, it may not come all that close. But that's okay! You'll improve quickly. And you may find that even a Modern Classroom lesson with ample room for improvement is more effective than a well-rehearsed traditional lesson. That's certainly what I found.

So when your videos contain mistakes, or your systems falter, or you just feel overwhelmed, take a deep breath—and take it easy on yourself too. You're human, and you're doing your best. That's all you can ever do. And you can always make things a little better tomorrow.

In my first year teaching in a Modern Classroom, I often struggled to find balance. I was excited about planning great lessons and developing great systems, which meant I sometimes worked long hours. But I found resources online that saved me work, accepted the fact that I'd often fall short of my own expectations, changed things up when necessary, and did my best to appreciate what was working well. That helped. And by my second year of implementation, when I had my lessons all planned and my course-level systems all built, teaching felt easier than ever before.

TEACHER TIP

DEVON McNALLY, MIDDLE SCHOOL MATH TEACHER (DURHAM, NORTH CAROLINA)

"The greatest piece of advice I can give is to do what you can, when you can. It can take a great deal of time to prepare and build all of the components when first implementing. It's okay to not have all the things in place when you start.

"Consider using a combination of assignments that can be auto-graded and those that require more time and energy on your part. Using the resources that are already created and available to you can also help protect your capacity as you build a collection of assignments.

"While the initial investment in planning and resource creation can be significant, remember that you don't need to do everything at once."

Takeaways: Your Journey Begins

If you're considering launching your own Modern Classroom, you're at an important moment in your teaching career. It's perfectly normal to feel nervous about adopting a new approach.

But while the model I've described may represent a big shift to your current practice, the steps I recommend you take are small. If you've followed the guidance in this book so far, in fact, you have everything you need to lead a classroom that meets every learner's needs. Now you just need to put it into action.

And that's exciting! Because when you do launch your Modern Classroom, you'll join thousands of educators, in schools around the world, who are using the same techniques to keep every learner appropriately challenged—and appropriately supported—every day. If these teachers can launch their Modern Classrooms, you can launch yours too. Both you and your students will benefit as soon as you do.

MASTERY CHECK

Before advancing to the next chapter, please make sure you understand how to:

☐ Explain how and when you will launch your Modern Classroom.

☐ Set students up for success with an effective self-paced orientation.

☐ Make teaching in a Modern Classroom sustainable.

Launching your Modern Classroom is a huge accomplishment. It's also just the beginning of your journey as a Modern Classroom educator. And if that journey is to be a long and fruitful one, as I hope it will be, you'll want to bring your community along with you.

Build Buy-In

If you believe Modern Classrooms can transform instruction, the first people you'll need to convince are your students. While orienting them during launch is a good start, what you really want is for every student to understand why you're teaching this way in the first place—and how it benefits them. If they believe Modern Classrooms are best for them too, they'll be eager to follow your lead.

Getting your students invested can also help you earn your community's trust and assistance. If you can get both your students' families and your administrators to support what you're doing, they can help you meet every learner's needs. But if they are confused about your purpose or expectations, you may struggle to get your Modern Classroom off the ground.

I firmly believe that change throughout a school community can begin with a single Modern Classroom. I've seen it happen many times! But for your classroom to have that kind of impact, you'll need to get your students, families, and administrators on board too.

CHAPTER OBJECTIVES

By the end of this chapter, you will be able to:

1. Explain how Modern Classrooms benefit students, families, and administrators.

2. Refine your approach through community input.

3. Respond effectively to pushback.

You've made it this far. How can you bring others along?

My Story: It Takes a Village

At first I was just testing new ways to meet David's and Anna's and Troy's needs. But as these practices evolved into a more coherent approach, people started asking me what I was doing, and why.

Sharing my Unit Zero was helpful. But even once they understood how my classroom worked, my students, their families, and my administrators still wanted to know: How exactly would my approach benefit them? Why wasn't I teaching the way they were used to? And what evidence, if any, did I have for this new approach?

I was initially surprised by their skepticism. It seemed obvious to me why this approach was better for my learners, so I thought it would be obvious to others too. It wasn't. But that was a good thing! These questions revealed genuine interest in my approach, and gave me the opportunity to explain my methods. Over time, I came to welcome them.

I also got better at responding. I learned to empathize with different stakeholders, and to explain the benefits of my approach in ways that resonated with each. I learned to acknowledge the perpetual challenges I faced—motivating students, fostering collaboration, simplifying systems and procedures—in a way that invited ideas and constructive feedback, rather than criticism. I learned what concerns my students, their families, and my administrators were most likely to raise, then figured out how to address them.

I didn't convince everyone. But over time, I won over most of my skeptics. My students came to appreciate the time they had to reach mastery, and the support I could offer each of them to get there. Their families came to appreciate the accessibility of my videos, and the extent to which I knew their children as human beings. And my administrators came to appreciate the quality of my data and the flexibility I offered my students. These stakeholders all came to understand, in other words, how Modern Classrooms met *their* needs too.

Earning this buy-in didn't happen overnight, nor was it easy. I had plenty of challenging conversations. But I always emerged from those conversations with new insights into both my students' and my community's needs. And once I knew better, I did better.

I don't think any Modern Classroom educator has ever implemented this approach without encountering confusion, concerns, and critique. But for every Modern Classroom educator, there are tens, hundreds, or maybe even thousands of community members—students, families, and administrators—who have come around to a new outlook on instruction. They've learned how Modern Classrooms work, and why they are better off in Modern

Classrooms than they were before. They have, in other words, bought in. And their schools better respond to students' needs as a result.

If you're ready to drive lasting change—in your classroom and beyond—you'll need to win over your community too. Here's what you can do.

Practice 10.1: Emphasize How This Benefits Others

A Modern Classroom will benefit you in many ways. But if you want others to buy in, you need to explain why your Modern Classroom is good for them too.

This shouldn't be too hard. Every person in your school building ultimately wants the same thing—for students to learn and grow— and if you can take the time to explain why your approach is good for students, you'll earn their support. Beyond the benefits for students, however, I've found that there are also certain aspects of the Modern Classroom approach that families and administrators find particularly compelling.[1] It's worth sharing them all!

Benefits for Students

At the start of the school year—and then whenever I felt it would be helpful for motivation—I told my students that, in my classroom:

◆ **"You'll really understand what I teach."** Young people want to understand things! I told my students explicitly that my goal wasn't just to cover content, but rather to make sure they mastered it. Even if students covered less, they would learn more.

◆ **"You'll have the time you need to learn."** Rushing through content is overwhelming for learners who aren't yet prepared

---

[1] Before you share with these stakeholders, you should also decide for yourself whether using the term *Modern Classroom* is helpful or not. The term is a useful shorthand for the comprehensive model it describes, and some stakeholders may appreciate knowing that these practices are backed by an organization that serves educators around the world. At the same time, many stakeholders are rightly skeptical of approaches that originate outside of their own school communities. Personally, I don't care whether you use the term or not. What I care about is giving you an approach that helps you meet your learners' needs—no matter what you call it.

to understand it. On the other hand, reviewing content at the teacher's pace is boring for students who already know it. I told my students that in my class they would always have something appropriately challenging to do—and that they could always move ahead as soon as they were ready.

◆ **"I'll be here to support you."** Learners want to feel seen, understood, and valued by their teachers. While accessing new content through videos might initially feel impersonal, I reminded my students that the purpose of my videos was actually to free me up, so that I could work closely with them throughout class. Once I digitized my direct instruction, I spent much more time with each of my learners—and got to know each much better as a result—than I ever had before.

◆ **"You can learn anytime, anywhere."** It's stressful for students to fall behind or miss class. So I reminded them that, if this ever happened, they could just watch my videos outside of school. They could always catch up—or, if they wanted, work ahead—whenever and wherever it worked best for them.[2]

My students were skeptical at first, but over time they realized that these claims were true. And when I heard my students repeating these benefits to the colleagues and administrators whom I often invited to visit my room, I knew my students understood what my Modern Classroom was all about.

TEACHER TIP

VICTORIA SCHULMAN, HIGH SCHOOL SCIENCE TEACHER (STAMFORD, CONNECTICUT)

"I have heard nothing but positive feedback about this approach. My students love having the videos that they can watch at their own speed—and rewatch if necessary. They also appreciate the many opportunities to try again if they need or want to, as well

---

[2] I required students to take Mastery Checks in school with me, which meant that students did need to show up to earn credit for their learning. But they could always catch up on several lessons at home and take the Mastery Checks for each of those lessons when they returned to class.

as the lack of a 'penalties for late work.' I tell the students that I understand that life happens, so my 'due dates' are just recommended pacing guides, and all they need to do is get the work completed before the end-of-unit test. In that way, I have relieved their anxiety about grades. Now my students are retaining more information, performing better, and doing so more happily and with less stress."

Benefits for Families

My students' parents and guardians cared primarily about their children's success, so explaining how my approach benefited students usually won families over. Nevertheless, there are two other benefits for families which I encourage you to share. In Modern Classrooms:

- ◆ **Families can engage directly with instruction.** In a traditional classroom, it can be hard for families to support student learning at home. Families may not know how their children's teachers have explained certain content, or they may not be familiar with the content in the first place.

  In my Modern Classroom, however, my students' families could watch my videos too! They could see exactly how I taught the content, then support their children in mastering it. I often heard from parents how much they enjoyed learning alongside their children.

- ◆ **It's clear what students do and do not yet know.** In a traditional classroom, it can be hard for a parent or guardian to discern what their child actually understands.

  In my Modern Classroom, however, I used Mastery Checks to assess each student's understanding of each content standard I taught. So when a parent or guardian checked my online gradebook, they could see exactly what their child had and had not yet mastered. They could celebrate their children's progress and encourage their children to keep on learning.

After a few years of sharing my approach with families, I noticed a pattern. At the start of each school year, parents and guardians were understandably nervous: this model was new to them, and they were concerned about the time their students spent on screens.

Many also worried that using computers in class would make learning feel impersonal and dull.[3]

Once they understood how my classroom actually worked, however, these parents and guardians were usually thrilled. (In fact, it's hard for me to remember a parent who truly understood this model and didn't like it.) They realized how well this approach would work for their children, and felt excited about the new ways in which they could support learning at home.

So whenever students' families asked to speak with me about Modern Classrooms, I was thrilled! I knew I'd have a chance to inform and empower these families—and I knew my students could get more support at home as a result.

TEACHER TIP

CANDI WILLIAMS, FIRST GRADE TEACHER (LOUISVILLE, KENTUCKY)

"I have a lot of very involved families and I knew there would be lots of questions regarding Modern Classrooms. So at our Open House, I held a class meeting where I explained the model to the families and showed them a short video of their children using MCP. They were all so impressed with what they saw that I received very few questions the rest of the year!"

Benefits for Administrators

When students are learning and families are engaged, administrators are usually pretty happy. Even so, Modern Classrooms offer administrators three other benefits worth sharing:

◆ **Modern Classrooms are data-driven.** Before I adopted the Modern Classroom model, I collected plenty of data. When I was delivering a single lesson to all of my students at once, however, I never really knew what to do with it.

---

[3] This is, unfortunately, a perception you may have to combat. You can remind people who are skeptical of instructional technology that, in your Modern Classrooms, videos simply free you up to spend more time interacting closely with your learners as human beings. There may well exist classrooms in which technology supplants human connection, but in Modern Classrooms technology is used to enhance it.

In my Modern Classroom, on the other hand, almost every decision I made—whether to let each student advance, what small-group mini-lessons to deliver, where students should sit, etc.—was shaped by real-time data on progress and mastery. My administrators, who believed strongly in the value of data-driven instruction, always appreciated that.

◆ **Modern Classrooms support the effective use of curriculum and technology.** Most schools and districts invest significant resources in purchasing curricula and tech tools for their teachers and students to use. It can be hard, however, for teachers to use these resources effectively. Standardized curricula, for instance, are rarely well-suited to the unique needs of any teacher's actual students.[4] And teachers often have so many school-provided tech tools at their disposal that they don't know where to begin.

Modern Classrooms don't require any particular curriculum or tech platform, but they do help teachers use what they already have more effectively. Self-paced courses, for instance, give students like Anna the time to engage deeply with the high-quality curriculum their schools provide, while learners like David can explore the rich extension activities at the end of each unit. And in digitizing direct instruction and organizing their learning management systems, Modern Classroom educators can leverage school-provided technology to enhance each of their lessons.

You may not teach every student every lesson of your curriculum—some may become Should-Do or Aspire-to-Do activities—nor use every tech tool at your disposal. Yet in giving each of your students the time and support they truly need to reach mastery, you will use those resources to their fullest pedagogical potential, thereby justifying the investments your administrators have made.

◆ **Modern Classrooms facilitate the delivery of other student-facing supports.** Many of my students received special-education services. It took a lot of work for my administrators

---

[4] The curricula I've seen are generally written for students with grade-level skills, even though the majority of American students lack grade-level proficiency. This puts teachers in a difficult position: they have great content to teach, but their students aren't prepared to understand it.

to ensure that these services were delivered effectively, especially in large general-education classrooms like mine.

Modern Classrooms, however, are designed to meet the unique needs of every learner—including learners with special needs. In several of my classes, for instance, I worked closely with a co-teacher certified in special education; whenever he needed, he could pull learners with individualized education programs (IEPs) aside to provide required support. He could use my videos to ensure that the supplemental instruction he provided outside of class aligned with what his students received from me. And when he needed to update students' progress toward IEP goals, the mastery data he needed was right on hand.

Whether students have IEPs or 504 plans, miss class for extracurricular or disciplinary reasons, or encounter other unique challenges, the flexibility that Modern Classrooms offer is invaluable for learners with special needs.

I found that my administrators, like my students' families, were initially hesitant about my approach. They had extensive experience and cared deeply about my students' learning, so it was natural for them to be skeptical of something new. But when I welcomed their questions, showed them what I was doing, and explained how this approach benefited them—and benefited my students, their families, and me personally—my administrators usually came around. In fact, they were often eager to show their peers what I was doing!

Teacher Tip

Andrea Mahr, Fifth Grade Teacher (Stanley, Wisconsin)

"My administrative team wasn't sold on it in the beginning, but once the scores of my students reflected that my class was even with or outperforming the other fifth-grade sections of students, they haven't expressed concern. I think it really helps that the videos my students watch are me teaching! If it weren't me, I would understand why they would have a lot of questions. But since I am creating the content and following the curriculum, I haven't had any issues."

Practice 10.2: Learn From Your Community

Sharing the benefits of Modern Classrooms will help you explain why your approach works. But if you really want the best possible Modern Classroom, you won't just see students, families, and administrators as people to convince. Instead, you'll solicit their input and use it to better meet their needs.

Running a Modern Classroom, like running any kind of classroom, will come with challenges. Students will fall behind, behavior incidents will occur, and you'll lose your patience. That's part of teaching. If you're pushing every student to be their very best, as you should, some struggles are inevitable.

So when these challenges do arise, it will be best for you—and for your learners—if you can lean on your community for support. You want your students to troubleshoot alongside you, their families to reinforce the messages you're sending in class, and your administrators to back you up. Here's how you can achieve that:

◆ **Get students' feedback.** Your students are your most important potential allies. If they feel like you're imposing the Modern Classroom approach against their wills, they may resist. If, on the other hand, they feel invested in the process of designing their own learning experiences, they'll feel both valued and accountable for their own success.

To some extent, of course, it's your job to tell students what to do: you're their teacher. But when you sit down with your learners and encourage them to reflect, you also have an opportunity to listen. I liked to ask my students, both during informal check-ins and on more formal end-of-unit reflections, two simple questions. First, what do you like about this class? And second, what might you change?

Sometimes these interactions provided actionable insights, and other times they didn't. That was okay. My students felt heard and valued, and they appreciated my openness to feedback even when it didn't lead immediately to change.

◆ **Send families updates.** You don't want families to learn about your approach only when their children struggle. If you aren't proactive, however, this can happen: a student falls behind, blames the way you teach, and leaves you needing to justify your approach.

To avoid this—and to help families reinforce the messages you're trying to send in school—it's best to let families know, as soon and as consistently as you can, what you're doing and why.

So every year, I collected as many parents' or guardians' email addresses as I could, then sent home a welcome message that included my Unit Zero materials. During back-to-school night and parent–teacher conferences, I explained to families both how they could access my LMS and how they could help their students learn outside of class. I wanted my students' families to see themselves as my partners in teaching their children—and the fact that my direct instruction was accessible online actually made this possible.

Then at least once per month, I sent home updates on students' progress, highlighting successes as well as opportunities for growth. With the data I had collected, I could easily share what each student had and had not yet mastered, where each student stood relative to pace, and what each student's specific next steps should be. I used a simple template to make sending these emails efficient.[5]

These messages may not reach every student's parent or guardian, and you may still receive complaints when students struggle. But being proactive helps families support their learners—and support you—throughout the year.

♦ **Invite administrators in.** It's always a good idea to let your school leaders know what you're doing in class, especially if you're doing something new. Your administrators' job is to help you succeed, and they can't do that if they don't understand what you're trying to achieve.

There are many ways you can share. You can schedule a meeting, send your administrators to MCP's website, or give them this book. What I really recommend, however, is that you invite them into your classroom. There's no better way for them to understand your approach than to see it in action.

Inviting others into your classroom can be scary, especially if you feel you're still figuring things out. But I've found that administrators genuinely appreciate being welcomed in.

---

[5] You can find customizable resources for communicating with families at www .meeteverylearnersneeds.org.

And if you're honest about what's going well and where you still see room for improvement, your administrators can give you meaningful feedback. I don't think I ever left a post-visit conversation without at least one idea for how I could improve. My relationships with my administrators always improved as well.

Finally, if your administrators like what you're doing—as I believe they will, once they understand it—they can help you share your approach with colleagues across your school or district. I'll discuss more ways to empower fellow teachers in the next chapter.

Sharing your approach with students, families, and administrators can be intimidating. When you open yourself up to feedback, you also invite critique, which can be hard to hear. But if that critique is based on incomplete or incorrect information, you can address the underlying misconception. And if that critique is well-informed, you can and should use it to improve.

So share what you're doing, be honest about why, and welcome feedback. The people you share with will appreciate being consulted, so they'll want to help you do better. And at the end of the day, involving your community in your classroom doesn't just benefit students, families, and administrators. It can benefit you, too.

TEACHER TIP

NOAH BEIGELMACHER, HIGH SCHOOL ELA TEACHER (NEW YORK, NEW YORK)

"My biggest piece of advice is to get as much feedback as you can from your students. When I launched my Modern Classroom I asked every week about what was going well and what wasn't. My students were able to see my blind spots: they made me aware of things that I didn't know were working, and told me the things they wanted more and less of.

"I didn't change everything they suggested but I did change a lot of things, and even when I didn't make changes their feedback allowed us to have a dialogue that helped us understand each other. So we reached a point where they could see where I was coming from, and they knew I would make some of the adjustments they asked for.

"So give yourself time to grow, talk to your students, and get feedback! It's not going to be perfect at first, but nothing is."

Practice 10.3: Prepare for Pushback

As I hope you'll agree, the case for Modern Classrooms is pretty compelling. But it can take time for students to realize the benefits I've described, and families and administrators may raise concerns about your approach before you have the time to explain it to them yourself.

So despite your best efforts to be proactive, it's inevitable that criticism will come. This is ultimately a good thing—criticism shows that stakeholders in your community care about what you're doing, and can lead to productive conversations—but that doesn't make it any easier to hear.

You can, however, make criticism easier to address by thinking ahead about the concerns you're most likely to hear—and how you'll respond to each. Over the years, I've found that people new to Modern Classrooms tend to raise three common critiques, each of which I believe you can effectively address:

♦ **"You aren't teaching."** I heard this often, especially early in the year. But the truth is that I was still teaching—just differently. In fact, given the time I spent crafting my lessons and the fact that my students could access my digital instruction anytime, anywhere, I was teaching *more* than I had before.

What students meant, I think, was that I was no longer delivering direct instruction live, and thus that they could no longer ask me questions in real time. After years of traditional instruction, they equated teaching with standing, delivering, and answering questions before the whole class.

In response, I explained to students that my videos were actually much clearer explanations than I could give in person: I worked hard to present my content as concisely as possible, and my videos were never interrupted by behavior challenges. In terms of answering questions, I was in fact *more* available than I'd been before: students could ask me questions throughout class, privately, without needing to pause a live lesson. They could use my whole-class tracker to find classmates to ask, too. And I could spend class engaged in the human work of teaching: getting to know my learners, then helping each unlock their full potential.

So to the extent that teaching involves explaining new things, I was explaining in a clearer and more accessible way. To the extent that teaching involves answering questions,

I was answering more questions in a more responsive way. And to the extent that teaching involves building relationships with learners, I was able to connect with each of my students—and foster authentic student-to-student collaboration—more effectively than I ever had before.

◆ **"I can't learn from videos."** Many learners understood how Modern Classrooms benefited students in general, but thought the model wouldn't work for them in particular. When this happened, trouble learning from videos was often a concern.

I admit my doubts about whether or not this was actually true: I know that my students often learned other things that mattered to them—songs or sports moves or video game tricks—on YouTube. But I took this concern in good faith, as you should too.

In response, I explained to my students that I didn't actually care how they learned. They could watch my videos—or not. They could ask their classmates. They could read textbooks, or search the Internet, or go on YouTube and find videos that were more engaging and better produced than mine. They could sit in on my live mini-lessons. And when they had questions about the content, they could ask me! How my students learned ultimately didn't matter: what mattered was that they achieved mastery. They had lots of ways to get there.

◆ **"This approach just doesn't work for me."** No matter how clearly or carefully you explain your approach, there will still be people who don't buy in. Although research shows that active engagement enhances learning, many students have grown so accustomed to sitting and listening that they believe that it's the approach that suits them best.[6]

---

[6] In one study conducted at Harvard University, students were randomly assigned to one of two classes: one that engaged students in active learning and another in which students received a lecture. Students reported more positive perceptions of learning from the lectures, but test scores showed that they had actually learned more through active engagement. See Deslauriers, L., McCarty, L. S., Miller, K., Callaghan, K., & Kestin, G. (2019). Measuring actual learning versus feeling of learning in response to being actively engaged in the classroom. Proceedings of the National Academy of Sciences of the United States of America, 116(39), 19251–19257.

In these cases, I always tried to ask students or their families: Was the one-size-fits-all model really working for you? And even if it was—which it usually wasn't—was it working for your classmates?

I didn't explicitly share the examples of David, Anna, or Troy. But if the student reminded me of David, I'd ask, "Isn't it boring when you can't advance?" If the student reminded me of Anna, I'd ask, "Isn't it frustrating when lessons assume knowledge you don't yet have?" And if the student reminded me of Troy, I'd ask, "Isn't it difficult to come back to class and get right back on track?" More often than not, the concerned student (or family member) got the point.

And there were days—if I had run out of time to prepare videos, for instance, or if I knew that all my learners needed to review a particular skill—when I would deliver a more traditional, teacher-led lesson. Most of the time, my students hated it! It may have just been that I wasn't a great lecturer. But once my students had a taste of self-paced learning, they were usually eager to get back to it—even the ones who had initially complained.

These are the most common concerns I've heard about Modern Classrooms, although they surely won't be the only ones. So whether you encounter these concerns or others, it's important that you listen and take them seriously, then find honest and empathetic ways to respond. Instruction really matters, so it's natural for your students, families, and administrators to question the way you provide it. You all have the same goal here—to help students learn—and it's important for everyone involved to feel heard.

In fact, I encourage you to see pushback as an opportunity. Every concern that's raised gives you the chance to connect with someone who cares about instruction, and to share with them what you believe is best. Conversations create change. And if you can leave those conversations better understanding how to meet your learners' needs, everyone will be better off.

Once they understand what you're doing and why, in fact, your critics may well become your strongest advocates.

TEACHER TIP

RACHEL PEACH, HIGH SCHOOL SCIENCE TEACHER (SYDNEY, AUSTRALIA)

"My biggest pushback has been from students and parents who want the comfort of a lecture from the front of the room. The change from traditional teaching to self-paced learning can be a big transition for some students, as students are still developing the habits they need to be successful and can feel defeated when they fail to reach mastery initially.

"In response I acknowledge that change is hard and empathize with students who are struggling, without giving in to their 'need' to return to what they like. To support them, I make sure to check in regularly, emphasize their wins whenever possible, and highlight the learning habits they are developing. Finally, I try to remind my students and families of the benefits of this pedagogy throughout the school year."

Takeaways: You Can Do This

I know this may sound daunting. Innovation is hard! And if you're introducing students, families, or administrators to this approach for the first time, you're on the front lines.

But if you've made it this far in this book, then I hope you'll agree: when it comes to our young people's education, this kind of innovation is necessary! The one-size-fits-all model fails millions of students every year, and we all suffer the consequences. When you bring Modern Classrooms to your community, therefore, you aren't just introducing a new method of instruction. You're taking a stand for what our young people—and our world—really need.

So stand tall! There are thousands of teachers around the world who have convinced their school communities that Modern Classrooms can meet every learner's needs, then used their communities' insights to meet those needs more effectively. And there are students, families, and administrators in each of these communities who have become passionate advocates for Modern Classrooms. If those teachers can do it, you can too.

MASTERY CHECK

Before advancing to the next chapter, please make sure you understand how to:

☐ Explain how Modern Classrooms benefit students, families, and administrators.

☐ Refine your approach through community input.

☐ Respond effectively to pushback.

Of course, leading change in your community is much easier if you can inspire your colleagues to join you. And innovation, it turns out, is just like learning: it's more fun, and ultimately more effective, if you can collaborate with friends. So once your students, families, and administrators have bought in, it's time to empower your peers.

Step 11

Empower Your Colleagues (Should-Do)

The entire Modern Classrooms Project is built on one simple idea: teachers learn best from one another.

That's how the Modern Classroom model was born, and it's how the Modern Classroom movement continues to grow. I learned how to create videos from Nick Bennett, then used Mastery Checks, progress trackers, and the other techniques I've described to meet my own learner's needs. Kareem learned that approach from me. Together, we built a nonprofit that empowers teachers to share these strategies with one another, no matter what or where they teach.

But sharing with teachers is not just how these techniques spread. It's also how they evolve! Every time I share this approach with another teacher, then watch what they do with it, I learn something new. I get better, and the Modern Classroom model does too.

So if you want to empower your colleagues—and improve in the process—I hope you'll join me in sharing what you've learned.

CHAPTER OBJECTIVES

By the end of this chapter, you will be able to:

1. Introduce Modern Classrooms in a way that invites other teachers' interest.

2. Inspire your colleagues to adopt and refine the Modern Classroom approach.

3. Support Modern Classroom implementation throughout your community.

The fundamental challenge of teaching affects every educator. But teachers are busy, and there are lots of instructional methods they can choose to learn. How do you convince your colleagues that the Modern Classroom model is worth their time—and help them implement it effectively once they decide that it is?

My Story: A Movement Grows at Eastern

Other teachers at Eastern were curious about what I was doing. So in my department and grade-level team meetings, I shared my approach. I showed my colleagues my videos and explained how I organized my LMS. My colleagues seemed impressed, but they were busy too. So while I may have given them useful tips about technology use, I didn't convince any of my peers to adopt my entire approach. Nor, at that point, was I really trying to.

Everything changed when I invited Kareem to my classroom. In a math department meeting about data-driven instruction, Kareem had noticed that while the rest of our colleagues felt stressed, I seemed relaxed. He was right! Analyzing data to determine the support each learner needed wasn't extra work for me. It was what I already did every day.

So I invited Kareem to observe one of my classes. This was new for me: while I often had administrators in my classroom, I had never really hosted other teachers. They were as busy as I was, and we often taught at the same times. But I taught during Kareem's lunch period, so he made the trip upstairs to visit my class.

The day Kareem visited was just a regular day of class. He walked around my room, spoke with my students, and asked me what program I used to record my videos. Then he left. That was that, I figured.

But the next day, Kareem asked me to visit his class during my lunch period. I did. And I was stunned: his students were already learning from videos! He had gone home the previous evening, recorded his first video, and shared it with his students. They already seemed deeply engaged.

We hadn't yet coined the term *Modern Classroom*, but suddenly there were two Modern Classrooms at Eastern.

That year—my third at Eastern—I was a finalist for our district's award for classroom innovation. I didn't win, but the next year Kareem did. His classroom was filmed, and he was honored at a district-wide awards ceremony.

When that happened, people noticed. Several of our Eastern colleagues saw the video of Kareem's classroom and asked if we could teach them our techniques. So that summer Kareem and I trained eight of our colleagues, who taught—and implemented our model effectively—in a variety of grade levels and content areas at Eastern. The Modern Classrooms Project was born.

The next summer, we trained 25 teachers across the DC area. That went well too, so we decided to post our training materials online. When COVID hit, interest skyrocketed. And once schools opened back up, the teachers we had trained—plus their students, families, and administrators—realized that our approach would remain effective for in-person learning too. (After all, that's what it was designed for!) MCP has only continued to grow since then.

It has taken a lot of time and hard work, and the contributions of many brilliant educators and advisors, to grow MCP into the organization it is today. But you don't need to start a nonprofit to empower your colleagues! There are simple things you can do, right away, to help other educators in your community meet their learners' needs. In fact, the reason the Modern Classroom movement exists is because thousands of educators have already taken those steps.

If you're ready to inspire your colleagues, here's what you can do.

Practice 11.1: Invite Your Colleagues In

Your colleagues are busy. They face countless demands on their time and attention. And they may be skeptical of approaches like ours, which promise to transform the way that instruction is delivered. There are plenty of fads in education—especially involving technology—and many ideas that sound promising. Unfortunately, there are far fewer practices that actually work.

So while you can certainly share this book, I believe that the best way to spark your colleagues' interest is to extend a personal invitation. Because teachers trust their peers, you can make the case for Modern Classrooms in your community more effectively than I can. You know your school; you know the challenges your students and colleagues face; and while I can explain this approach in writing, you can show your colleagues how it actually works in practice. That makes you the best person to inspire your colleagues.

Here are a few ways to spark their interest:

♦ **Present at a staff meeting or professional development (PD).** I learned about instructional videos at Nick's brief presentation. He wasn't pitching anything: he was just sharing a practice that worked for his students. Presenting at our district's PD day was a nice opportunity for him, and a chance to connect with like-minded peers: he and I stayed in touch after that presentation, and continued to exchange ideas that helped both of us grow.

  If you can present at a staff meeting or PD, you can find presentation materials at meeteverylearnersneeds.org. But you don't actually need special resources or support! All you really need to do is explain, in an authentic and personal way, what you're doing, why you're doing it, and how your colleagues can learn more.

♦ **Share what you've created so far—both as a resource and for feedback.** I had encountered instructional videos before, but I never realized they were something that I could actually create. Seeing Nick's actual videos—which weren't fancy, and which I realized I could emulate—changed that. He wasn't a professional video creator, after all. He was a teacher just like me.

  Nick also shared his videos in two ways that encouraged me to engage. First, he shared them as a resource: he told us that, if we wanted to use his videos with our own students, we could. And second, he asked for our feedback. He wanted to get better, and was legitimately interested in our ideas for how he could do that.

  We teachers love ready-made resources—videos, Mastery Checks, progress trackers, etc.—and everyone likes being asked for their advice. So if you can share what you've created as both a resource and an invitation for feedback, I think your colleagues will appreciate you too.

♦ **Welcome classroom visits.** Finding time for colleagues to visit can be difficult, and opening your classroom to peers can feel vulnerable. But it's also, in many ways, the easiest way to share your approach—you just have a colleague in your room while you do your thing. As Kareem's experience suggests, the best way to understand a Modern Classroom is to see one in action.

And if your colleague(s) can visit, try your best to find a time afterward to debrief. This is a good way for you to share more about your approach, answer questions, and collect feedback on what you can improve. The discussions I had with Kareem after he observed my classroom led us to create MCP!

◆ **Recommend resources you have found useful.** You don't have to explain everything yourself: you can direct your colleagues online to learn more! Consider sharing this book, the supplemental resources available at meeteverylearnersneeds.org, and/or MCP's online courses. The guidance that has helped you will help your colleagues. You learned and implemented this approach, after all, so your colleagues can too.

However you choose to share, make sure you explain not just what you're doing, but also why. How is a Modern Classroom making your life easier? How is it helping your students learn? If your colleagues understand the benefits you experience, they'll naturally want to understand how your classroom works.

So reach out! Be welcoming, be honest, and be brave. And once you can convince a few other teachers to take the leap with you, you can start supporting each other.

TEACHER TIP

ARACELI CALLE FERNANDEZ, K-8 SPANISH TEACHER (SOLLENTUNA, SWEDEN)

"Discovering MCP was transformative because it gave me clear strategies and resources to individualize teaching. After completing the online course, I integrated MCP principles into my classes.

"I then talked to my principal about the model, who liked it and spread information about it in her newsletter. I've also shared MCP ideas with colleagues and other language teachers through discussions and a blog post (in Swedish). While I haven't presented the model formally yet, several colleagues have adopted its strategies such as making instructional videos.

"For me MCP is more than a pedagogical method; it is also a global community where teachers can learn, share ideas, and support each other in delivering high-quality, individualized education."

Practice 11.2: Support Each Other

It's possible for any teacher anywhere to launch a Modern Classroom on their own. I know many who have! But as with anything, it's easier to create change with a group of thoughtful, committed colleagues. Learning and launching Modern Classrooms alongside your peers can help you reflect on successes and struggles, troubleshoot common challenges, and hold each other accountable. I've seen small groups of teachers accomplish big things.

The daily grind of teaching can make this kind of collaboration difficult, especially with colleagues who teach different subjects or grade levels than you do. You probably spend much of the day in your own classroom, and after class ends I'm sure you have plenty more to do.

Yet if you're resourceful, there are ways you can bring like-minded colleagues together for discussion and collaboration. It might mean starting a professional learning community (PLC), if your school has time set aside for teacher-led PD. It might be meeting during lunch once or twice per month. It might even just be starting an email thread or group chat, then sharing questions and ideas there. You'll know better than I will what will work in your community. But I know that where there's a will, there's a way.

However you form this group, I encourage you to:

◆ **Celebrate successes.** Teachers who are interested in the Modern Classroom model may initially feel intimidated by it. And once they launch, these teachers may feel insecure about their implementation. There's so much to develop and refine, especially at the beginning, that it can feel impossible to do everything effectively.

   In my experience, the best way to inspire hesitant colleagues—and to encourage those just starting out—is to celebrate moments of success, both from your classroom and from theirs. Did you create a fun video recently? Have a nice interaction with a learner you had been struggling to reach? Or even just see a student smile after achieving mastery? If so, share what you've accomplished—even if it feels small—and encourage your colleagues to do the same. Hearing about those small wins will motivate your colleagues, and make them feel like they can succeed too.

◆ **Troubleshoot common challenges.** When your colleagues launch Modern Classrooms, they'll surely hit obstacles. They'll have lots of planning to manage, for instance, and students to motivate. They may not know how to handle these challenges. And if they don't find a way, they may give up before they or their students can experience this model's benefits.

If you've encountered similar hurdles, you can share how you've overcome them; if not, you can lead a reflective discussion that helps your colleagues—and you—arrive at workable solutions. The more you can get teachers talking to each other here, the better the solutions you'll be able to find.

◆ **Plan together.** The best instructional resources you can find may well be your colleagues down the hall. If colleagues who teach your same courses are interested in implementing Modern Classrooms, you can still share the work of lesson planning and video creation.[1] And if your colleagues who implement Modern Classrooms teach different courses, you can still share general resources like progress trackers, LMS tips, and reflection forms. Creating consistent systems across Modern Classrooms at your school can also make things easier for students who take multiple Modern Classroom courses.

◆ **Offer feedback and affirmation.** It may not be your job to provide your colleagues feedback, but it is an opportunity: you can offer honest critiques and suggestions without the stress of formal observations. You can offer to visit their classrooms (if schedules permit) or to review their lesson or unit materials. You'll learn from doing this, too! And if you're open to it, you can share how your classroom works—and model openness to feedback—by inviting visits and/or feedback from your colleagues.

When you do provide feedback, it's equally important to affirm what your colleagues are trying to do. Taking risks is

---

[1] I've often seen colleagues who teach the same courses divide up video creation so that each teacher creates some of the videos. I think this works really well: these teachers can all tailor instruction to the needs of students in their school community, and it creates nice variety for students too. If you choose to use other videos instead—which also works!—then you and your colleagues can work together to find good ones.

never easy! A few kind words can mean a great deal to colleagues who doubt themselves. Consider the way you encourage your students—with empathy and care—and give your peers the same kind of support.

◆ **Be open and inviting.** Not every teacher at your school may be familiar with the Modern Classroom model. That's okay. Invite them to join your discussions anyway! Newcomers may bring valuable questions and ideas, even if they don't end up implementing right away. And a greater diversity of perspectives—in terms of demographics, subjects and grade levels taught, prior experiences, etc.—can only enrich your conversation.

I also encourage you to include your administrators. As I explained in the previous chapter, it's good for everyone if your leaders know what you are doing—and these leaders are likely to offer valuable insights as well. Besides, what administrator doesn't like to see a group of committed educators working together to improve their practice?

Every Modern Classroom is, ultimately, its own laboratory for innovation. The more educators you can gather, the more insights you can generate, and the more every teacher—no matter their level of implementation—can learn. So get your colleagues together! That's exactly how the Modern Classrooms Project got started. And you never know where your own discussions may lead.

Finally, if leading a group like this sounds like a lot of work, it doesn't need to be. You can find dedicated guidance for PLC leaders at meeteverylearnersneeds.org, as well as other free resources to guide your discussion. All you need to do is bring your colleagues together.

TEACHER TIP

LAURIE HUTCHINSON, HIGH SCHOOL ELA TEACHER (DALLAS, TEXAS)

"When I discovered MCP's ideals, principles, and processes, it nearly stopped me in my tracks. I was so excited that I gathered my team and promptly started figuring out how to weave videos, self-pacing, and mastery learning into our lessons. Immediately, a teammate and I took MCP's free online course and began re-designing our curriculum. Within three months, the rest of the team was onboard.

"We team plan all of our assignments, meeting first to determine big-picture goals structured around the pacing tracker, then developing and adjusting our curriculum to split up the work and make light (or lighter) the work of assembling the unit to post in Google Classroom. This process serves our team very well, and our students consistently outperform the district on several metrics.

"Now I talk about MCP with everyone and anyone who will listen because teachers are hungry for a different way of teaching."

Takeaways: One Classroom at a Time

When I started redesigning my lessons during my first year at Eastern, I never intended to inspire other teachers. I was just trying to make it through each day without feeling like a failure.

But my approach worked for me. When I used it I felt more relaxed, and colleagues like Kareem noticed. I answered Kareem's questions, and helped him make my approach his own. Before long, our colleagues were asking both of us how we did it.

So this is how Modern Classrooms spread at Eastern, then across our district, and subsequently in communities across the country and world: as a movement of teachers working together to improve instruction, one classroom at a time. When teachers are empowered to learn and innovate together, entire communities benefit.[2]

And if I can inspire Kareem, then Kareem and I can inspire teachers around the world, then you can inspire your colleagues too. You just need to invite their interest, then support them in learning more. That may not sound like much, but it's enough to redesign instruction.

---

[2] For the past two decades, education researcher John Hattie's *Visual Learning* studies have synthesized thousands of meta-analyses exploring the impacts of more than 200 different influences on student learning outcomes. Collective teacher efficacy—in other words, the shared belief among teachers that they can positively impact student achievement—has consistently been one of the influences on student learning outcomes. See Hattie, J. (2012). Visible Learning for Teachers: Maximizing Impact on Learning. London: Routledge.

MASTERY CHECK

Before advancing to the next chapter, please make sure you understand how to:

☐ Introduce Modern Classrooms in a way that invites other teachers' interest.

☐ Inspire your colleagues to adopt and refine the Modern Classroom approach.

☐ Support Modern Classroom implementation throughout your community.

Meeting your own learners' needs is a great accomplishment, and inspiring others to do the same is an incredible feat. But it's a big, complex world—and there are larger systems that shape what you and your colleagues can achieve. If you're up for it, I think you can help improve those systems too.

Step 12

Shape the Conversation (Aspire-to-Do)

If you redesign your lessons and courses, you'll make teaching more enjoyable—and sustainable—for yourself. If you can get your students and community to buy in, you'll help young people like David, Anna, and Troy build authentic mastery and deserved self-esteem. And if you empower your colleagues, you'll multiply your impacts. The changes you and your colleagues make within your classrooms' walls will benefit your students and community for years to come.

Yet if you focus only on what happens in your and your colleagues' classrooms, there's a limit to how much you can change.

No matter how you teach, your classrooms exist within a larger education system. Who, when, and what you teach are policy decisions, made and shaped by a complex network of administrators, elected officials, philanthropists, and researchers. These policy decisions influence every pedagogical choice you make. And the challenges these policies inevitably create—the challenges that feel beyond your control—affect your colleagues and students too.

So at some point, once your Modern Classroom is up and running, you may want to consider how you can help redesign the system too. And you should! You know your students better than anyone else does, and you're the person whose actions ultimately translate policy into practice. A policy that won't work for you won't work.

And while there are many decisions that I think you can and should attempt to influence, there are a few places where I think your perspective as a Modern Classroom educator can be particularly valuable—especially if you'd like to live in a world that meets every learner's needs.

CHAPTER OBJECTIVES

By the end of this chapter, you will be able to:

1. Explain how school and district policies affect students' and teachers' daily experiences.

2. Identify policy changes that can help teachers meet every learner's needs.

3. Advocate for the policies you believe are best.

Contributing to larger systemic discussions can feel intimidating, and you've certainly got more immediate concerns. But your students and colleagues need policies, just like lessons and courses, that meet their diverse needs. And if you don't advocate for what you know works, who will?

My Story: Taking a Stand

In my third year at Eastern, I had an opportunity. A local nonprofit called Teaching for Change offered a writing workshop for teachers interested in sharing their stories. As I imagine you've gathered, I like to write. So I enrolled.

I had no idea what I wanted to write about. But I thought about the challenges I hadn't yet been able to address, and landed on something I wanted to change: my district's new grading policy.

That year, my district had quietly adopted a policy that gave students partial credit on their transcripts for failing grades. This policy made it easier for students like Anna and Troy to graduate, but I felt that it lowered expectations for students, making it harder for me and my colleagues to require understanding.

The district's grading policy was beyond my control, but I nevertheless saw an opportunity to influence it. I knew more rigorous expectations, based on mastery, would both motivate my learners in school and better prepare them for life afterward. And I felt compelled to advocate for a grading policy that would meet every learner's needs, not just in my own classroom but across learners' academic careers.

So I wrote an article explaining my experience with the district's new policy, and it was published in a local newspaper.[1]

---

[1] Barnett, Robert. "A D.C. Teacher's Bold Vision to Improve Scandalously Poor Student Performance." *Washington City Paper*, May 18, 2017.

My article didn't change the district's grading policy overnight. Yet I know from the notes I received after publication—including several from district staff—that it informed decision-makers' thinking. After other teachers and journalists expressed similar concerns, the district eventually did revisit its policies. And many of the ideas I developed in that article continue to inform my and MCP's work today.

I'm proud of that article. I'm also proud to say that over the past several years, Modern Classroom educators across the world have taken similar stands. They've written articles, presented at conferences, and appeared in the news or on podcasts to share what they believe.[2] They are transforming our system, one classroom at a time.

If you're ready to join us in building a world where every learner can succeed, here are some things you can do.

Practice 12.1: Request Time to Learn and Autonomy to Implement

I believe that every educator in the world can benefit from learning the Modern Classroom model. Whether they choose to adopt our methods fully, partially, or not at all, exploring the techniques I've described in this book can only empower teachers and the students they serve.

Learning these practices, however, takes time. Teachers need time to understand our approach, time to create videos and Mastery Checks and progress trackers, and time to reflect on what's working and refine what isn't. This time, for teachers, is precious: there's always so much to do. But when schools and districts can set aside additional time for professional development—and, if possible, compensate teachers for participating—I believe that's time and money well-spent. It certainly increases the chances that teachers will implement research-backed models like ours effectively.

To innovate in ways that meet every learner's needs, teachers also need autonomy. Teachers need the freedom to try new things, and the discretion to adapt and iterate over time. And because individual teachers know their own students better than

---

[2] You can see how Modern Classroom educators are shaping the conversation—and explore ways to do the same—at meeteverylearnersneeds.org.

policymakers do, policymakers should trust and support teachers to apply the research-backed approaches those teachers think are best. This empowers teachers as professionals, and supports instruction that is tailored to what students actually need.

Giving teachers this autonomy, of course, means that some may learn the Modern Classroom approach and choose not to implement it. But that's how it should be! Much as I believe that this model is the right way to educate our young people—it's how I want my own kids to learn—I believe even more strongly that individual teachers know what works best for themselves and for their students. I want every teacher on Earth to understand this approach, but I don't expect that every teacher will use it. Nor do I want any teacher to be required to. Teachers should choose how they teach.

So what does this all mean for you? In a conversation with your principal, a letter to your superintendent, a grant proposal to a local foundation, or even an upcoming teacher's union meeting (if applicable), I encourage you to advocate for both time and autonomy. Share that you want to learn new techniques, but that doing so takes time. And explain that to truly meet your learners' needs, you'll need the freedom to do what you think is best—whether that involves Modern Classroom practices or not. If you can convince your leaders to provide that, I'm confident that you, your colleagues, and most importantly your students will all benefit.

TEACHER TIP

AIMEE YOCOM, MIDDLE SCHOOL SOCIAL STUDIES TEACHER (ANTELOPE, CALIFORNIA)

"I first approached my colleagues and my administrators in the spring. I shared MCP's videos and data to gain their buy-in. The next year, all eighth-grade social studies teachers decided to adopt this model.

"I made it my mission to visit with my admin once a month to share what was going on in my room. I also invited them to visit often, as my door was always open. I then reached out to the district curriculum department and asked to conduct a Professional Learning Institute, which was five after school sessions to introduce the model to anyone interested. I had ten teachers attend from second grade to eighth grade.

"The next year, I worked with MCP and my admin to push for more district support. Prior to this, the district's curriculum department had been hesitant, believing this model only works for high achievers. However, we convinced my district that it works for everyone, and now we have a partnership with MCP, so that more teachers can learn this model.

"I will continue to push for more support, but most of all, I really appreciate that my district is not forcing everyone to adopt the model. They are supporting the model for those that want to take the leap."

Practice 12.2: Make Mastery the Goal

Even if teachers can learn and implement our approach, school and district policies shape how effective their implementation can be. The more these policies emphasize understanding, the more your Modern Classroom can foster it. And I believe that the goal of any education policy, like the goal of any lesson or course, should be to support learner understanding.

If you look closely at many school or district policies, however, you'll realize that they have competing goals. Grading policies that reward participation, for instance, encourage students to behave in certain ways—but students can behave well without understanding, or behave poorly and understand. Standardized testing policies produce aggregate data that's used to evaluate teachers and schools—but students' individual scores often have little impact on the instruction these individual students receive. And policies that award students credit based on the number of hours they spend in class, rather than the understanding they've shown, reward attendance—but send students like Anna to advanced classes unprepared to succeed. These policies all make some sense. But none of them prioritizes mastery.

Because the goal of any Modern Classroom is to help students master content and skills, I believe that Modern Classrooms can be most effective in schools and districts where grading, assessment, and credit policies emphasize understanding. Practically, speaking, this means a few things:

◆ **Students' grades should reflect their actual understanding.** Many policies require that teachers grade things like participation and homework. These grades often reflect a student's discipline, work ethic, and home life more than they indicate understanding. A student like Anna, after all, can participate in class or complete a homework assignment without achieving mastery, especially if she has help at home. If David already understands the content, on the other hand, he might not feel motivated to pay attention or do homework.

These grades may encourage desirable behaviors, but they can also obscure the true goal of mastery. The reason why participating and working hard are desirable in the first place is because they help students achieve understanding—so that's where the focus should be. Using objective criteria for mastery reduces the potential impact of teacher bias on grades as well.

Ultimately, students' grades should reflect what they understand—not how they behave. So I encourage you to advocate for grading policies that put mastery first.

◆ **Students should be assessed—and reassessed—when they are ready.** In many schools, students spend weeks of school preparing for, taking, and then decompressing after standardized assessments. This is a tremendous investment of valuable learning time. Yet for learners like David, Anna, and Troy, it's not clear that these tests are worth the effort. If Anna can fail year after year of standardized tests yet advance regardless, what's the point?

Eliminating standardized testing altogether seems impractical. But so is wasting all those hours of student and teacher time! A better approach would limit the time students spend testing, allow students to take such tests—like Mastery Checks—when they are ready, and ensure that the data these tests generate is used, as quickly as possible, to adjust the instruction that individual students receive.[3] And if students

---

[3] For a student like Anna, I imagine that taking standardized tests each year feels like going to the hospital every May, spending a week there feeling sick, and then being told every October only that her health is poor. Testing students' understanding as a means of evaluating schools and teachers isn't unreasonable, but the real purpose of these tests should be to diagnose students' weaknesses so that they can be remedied. If Anna fails her year-end tests but moves on to the next grade regardless—and without significant intervention—then the tests have wasted her time and effort.

fail an assessment, we should—if we actually care that they learn the material—give them the chance to try again.

Offering students realistic chances to succeed, using test results to determine next steps, and requiring students to achieve mastery will make assessment a better use of both students' and teachers' precious time.

◆ **Students should earn credits by demonstrating high levels of understanding.** In secondary settings, students advance through school by accumulating credits. Too often, however, students receive these credits based on the number of hours they've spent sitting in a particular course and/or an arbitrary grade-based threshold, such as the requirement that a student receive at least a D average (usually around 65%) in order to pass a class. David, Anna, and Troy, for instance, each received the same credit for their ninth-grade Algebra 1 class, even though David understood the content and Anna and Troy did not.

Using in-seat hours (also known as Carnegie units) and passing grades (D or higher) to award credits is bad for students. For David, the requirement that he spend a full year in Algebra 1 prevented him from learning as much as he could have: if he had been allowed to master the content more quickly, he could have moved straight ahead to more challenging content. At the same time, letting Anna and Troy advance beyond Algebra 1 with incomplete understandings set them up to fail in Algebra 2. Even if their passing grades reflected their true mastery of the content—which, given their below-proficient scores on year-end standardized tests, seems unlikely—it's hard to argue that a student who understands 65% of Algebra 1 is truly ready to move on.

Students' grades can be inflated or manipulated, but their understanding cannot. So awarding full course credit for partial understanding sends the wrong message about the purpose of school: students focus on simply getting by, rather than mastering new things. More importantly, passing unprepared students from grade to grade creates learning gaps that set students up to fail in the future, and makes it difficult—at least in traditional classrooms—for students who miss key concepts to catch back up.

Raising the bar to pass may seem, in the short term, painful: we will make it harder for students to graduate. Yet keeping expectations low, in the long run, is worse: we let students like Anna and Troy reach high school without mastering even basic math and reading skills. And in doing so, we damage both their career prospects and their self-esteem. We can't keep letting that happen!

Instruction, ultimately, should help every student achieve mastery. And because grading, assessment, and credit policies determine how teachers spend their time—and how students prioritize theirs—it's important that these policies emphasize real understanding. So if your school's or district's policies don't yet emphasize mastery, I encourage you to advocate for policies that do. It will support what you're doing in your Modern Classroom, and thereby help every student succeed.

TEACHER TIP

PERLA LUJAN, HIGH SCHOOL ELA & Social Studies TEACHER (MEXICO CITY, MEXICO)

"I spoke informally with my colleagues about Modern Classrooms and then invited my colleagues to learn more. They were interested because it fit into my school's vision of student empowerment and collaboration, and they wanted to help students be more independent learners. When they saw how much my students had learned, and how simple my progress trackers and Mastery Checks were, they decided to implement these practices themselves.

"Now we all use the same grading policy: students must achieve a score of 8/10 or higher to advance. Just as important, we give students the chance to reassess as many times as needed, and help students use their practice to find the gaps in their learning. Now students always know where to go and what to do if they need to revise, and they have lots of opportunities to talk to their teachers and peers about how they can improve."

Practice 12.3: Reconsider Age–Based Promotion

This book attempts to answer one very difficult question: how can one teacher simultaneously meet David's, Anna's, and Troy's needs? I have asked and tried to answer it because it's a question that teachers around the world must ask themselves every day. But there's a larger question worth asking too. Why are David, Anna, and Troy even in the same precalculus class at all?

The obvious answer is that David, Anna, and Troy are roughly the same age. They were born within the same one-year span, and their bodies and brains have had the same amount of time to develop. They probably started formal schooling around the same time, and they've moved together from grade to grade, starting in kindergarten and ending up with me.

There are logical reasons to organize students in this way. For instance, it seems safe: young people spend their days around peers of roughly the same size and social–emotional maturity. It creates economic predictability: students spend most of their time in school until they turn eighteen, at which point they are eligible—and, at least in theory, prepared—to enter the workforce or pursue higher education. It feels fair: David, Anna, and Troy all get to see the same amount of content in the same amount of time. Finally, it's what we're all used to. This, we think, is just how school works.

From a learning perspective, however, this age-based approach is neither equitable nor efficient. And it doesn't really work! David and Anna may both be seventeen, but their mathematical knowledge and ability are many years apart. Their physical and social-emotional development may be too. And while Troy has been enrolled in school for as many years as David and Anna, he has been present much less often. The vast differences in these same-age young people's academic needs—which Modern Classrooms can address but not ultimately cure—are what makes teaching so difficult in the first place.

For teachers and students stuck in this age-based system, the end of any academic year presents a series of bad choices. It doesn't feel right to hold Anna back: it's not her fault that she was unprepared, not clear that a second time through the content will go any better, and not good for her college or career prospects. I could recommend David for an advanced class and Anna for a remedial one, but this doesn't seem fair either: placing them on separate academic "tracks" may prevent Anna from ever reaching advanced math material, no matter how hard she works, and may reinforce the message that she's not really capable of understanding math anyway. I could suggest that both of them pursue extra-curricular math activities over the summer—David for enrichment, Anna for support—but this may not be possible or productive for either.

So teachers like me usually pass students like David, Anna, and Troy along, hoping that next year they'll learn more. And if they're in Modern Classrooms next year, they might! In a Modern Classroom, all three of these students can be appropriately challenged and supported every day.

Yet Modern Classrooms have their limitations too. If David starts the year far ahead of Anna and they both work hard all year, Anna may still end the year far behind. The larger problem is that our system still expects these students, who happen to be the same age, to learn the exact same things in the exact same amount of time. In an age-based system, gaps like these inevitably form and continue to grow—even in Modern Classrooms.

The better approach, it seems to me, would be to advance learners like David and Anna through school itself—as in a Modern Classroom—based on what they do and do not yet understand. If David can learn sixth-grade math in three months, he should progress to seventh-grade math right away. And if Anna needs two years to master the same content, she should take those two years! Once she actually has what we consider sixth-grade skills, she'll be prepared to master seventh grade too, rather than sitting through many more years of math class she isn't prepared to understand.

A system like this, which prioritizes students' understanding over their age, strikes many people as impractical. We're so used to age-based classes, in which students spend every year learning together at the same pace, that it's hard to imagine a world in which students do anything else. Could we really have classes with students of different ages, learning different things at the same time?

Strange as this may initially seem, I actually don't see why we couldn't. Young people can and should learn to interact with schoolmates of different ages, and Modern Classrooms demonstrate that students working on different lessons within the same course can nevertheless support and engage with one another. People often raise cases that seem absurd—would a seven-year-old be in the same class as a seventeen-year-old?—but I think those are easily addressed: we could keep students in elementary and middle and high schools based on their age, while making instruction within those schools as flexible as possible. Sure, we might see fourteen-year-olds in the most advanced high school classes, and eighteen-year-olds in the most basic. But students of those ages already interact regularly in high schools anyway—in clubs and electives and teams and hallways—so I don't see an obvious reason to keep them apart. And while there might be some stigma around being an older student in a more basic math class, I think it's preferable to being stuck in a math class one can't possibly understand. There's also a plausible pathway out: work hard, learn the material with teacher and classmate support, and advance to the next class!

I don't know, logistically speaking, exactly how this would work. It might require shifts to school staffing, scheduling, and/or assessment practices. It might require teachers to teach certain sets of standards, instead of yearlong cohorts of same-age students, and students to move from teacher to teacher multiple times throughout the school year.[4] It might even require us to rethink the concept of age-based "grade levels" altogether. Like a Modern Classroom, it might initially be uncomfortable for teachers, students, families, and administrators.

But if we look at the system we have now, I think we should all agree—teachers, students, families, administrators—that it fails to meet every learner's needs. It holds David back from achieving his potential, rushes Anna through content she is unprepared to master, and effectively ignores Troy's attendance challenges. It squanders all of their potential in the process.

Ultimately, I believe that we should take what's working in Modern Classrooms and apply that approach to school itself. We should find ways for schools at large to give every student the time they need to learn, and the support required to learn as much as possible. I don't know exactly how this will work. But if you agree with me here, as I hope you will, then I also hope you'll join me in seeking solutions.

And in the meantime, we'll have Modern Classrooms.

TEACHER TIP

ISAAC MUREITHI, UNIVERSITY PROFESSOR (NYERI, KENYA)

"I was so captivated by the potential of Modern Classroom that I founded Faiyol Academy in 2021, utilizing this cutting-edge teaching method for our instruction. For several years now, my

---

[4]Rather than having two Geometry teachers who teach the same content over the course of a year, for instance, a school might make one teacher responsible for the first half of Geometry and the other teacher responsible for the rest. Students would move from the first teacher to the second when ready.

teachers and administrators have been trained to use Modern Classrooms—a technique that has completely transformed education at our school.

"It has been remarkable using the Modern Classroom model for our pre-K to elementary students, allowing us to create captivating lessons and observe their progress in real time. I am proud that this method has improved teaching quality by making it more involved and dynamic."

Takeaways: The David–Anna–Troy Test

The ideas I've outlined in this chapter are just a few examples of policies that can help teachers meet every learners' needs. I'm sure there are other opportunities to redesign systems in ways that support Modern Classroom instruction—and I encourage you to pursue them all! If you notice things beyond your control that make your job hard, like the grading policy I had to implement at Eastern, I hope you'll suggest changes that make teaching and learning easier.

And if you're ever wondering whether a particular policy will benefit all learners, then I encourage you to ask three simple questions:

1. Will this policy help David?

2. Will this policy help Anna?

3. Will this policy help Troy?

If you believe that a particular change to your school or district policies would help you challenge David, support Anna, and help Troy catch up, then I believe you should advocate for that change. If, on the other hand, you believe that a proposed change will enshrine a one-size-fits-all model that truly fits none, or meet some students' needs but not others, you should also speak up: that change will only widen inequality.

As a teacher of students like David, Anna, and Troy, you understand these policies' impacts better than anyone. So take a stand! Your students, colleagues, and community will be better off when you do.

MASTERY CHECK

You've almost finished Part 3 of this book! Before advancing to the conclusion, please make sure you understand how to:

☐ Explain how school and district policies affect students' and teachers' daily experiences.

☐ Identify policy changes that can help teachers meet every learner's needs.

☐ Advocate for the policies you believe are best.

Redesigning our education system may seem impossible. But it's worth remembering that our school system is, at its core, just a lot of educators like you, leading a lot of lessons, in a lot of courses over a lot of years.

So if we can redesign lessons and courses, as thousands of Modern Classroom educators already have, we can redesign instruction too. We can do this by advocating for policies that meet every learner's needs. And with the support of our students and families and administrators, we can continue to build a brighter future, one classroom at a time.

Modern Classrooms are not perfect. They are different from what many of us are used to—that's part of the point—and take time and hard work to implement effectively. They address but don't ultimately cure the larger problems of age-based education in an unequal world. And like any approach, they create their own challenges. I hope my story has been clear about that.

Yet I hope my story has also been clear about the opportunity we possess. Our schools are full of students with infinite potential. Our teachers, administrators, families, and policymakers care deeply about doing what is best. And there really is a way to meet every learner's needs! I've done it, the teachers quoted throughout this book have done it, and you can do it too.

Our young people, our communities, and our shared future depend on you.

Conclusion: Change Starts Every Day

Ten years before I started writing this book, I finished my first year teaching at Eastern. The Modern Classroom model had started to take shape. What I was doing back then wasn't nearly as polished as what I've presented in this book—it has taken a decade of hard work and the insights of many brilliant educators to get here—but the foundations were all in place.

When I think of all that has happened since then—meeting Kareem, co-founding MCP, and seeing educators around the world use our model to meet their learners' needs—I feel proud. Every teacher faces the same fundamental challenge, and I'm glad that what worked for me is working for others too.

I also feel concerned. There are millions of Davids in our schools, millions of Annas, and millions of Troys. These are young people with their whole lives ahead of them, and if we don't meet their needs now, we will squander their potential. That's unfair to those students and a loss for the world. Every young person deserves to be appropriately challenged—and appropriately supported— every day.

Educators also deserve a new approach. The teachers I meet care deeply about doing what's best for students, then work long and often thankless hours to provide that. Yet if they aren't able to meet their learners' diverse needs, they may burn out. You might too. That's not good for anyone.

If you're willing to try something new, however, then I hope you'll take heart. There are simple things you can do, right away, to give every learner the challenge and support they need! I used these practices in my own classroom, I've seen thousands of educators use them in theirs, and I know you can adopt them in your classroom too. They are small steps that make a big difference. And I hope, both for your and your students' sakes, that you will take them.

Here's what I recommend you do.

Modernize an Upcoming Lesson

I've covered a lot here. I've explained how you can redesign your lessons, transform your courses, and lead the Modern Classroom movement in your own community. I think you should do all these things! But they all take time—and you've already got plenty to do.

So I urge you: start small. Remember that everything I've described here began with a single lesson, on composite functions. And that's also where you should begin: with a single Modern Classroom lesson, which you can plan in less than an hour. I saw the benefits right away, and I'm confident you will too.

All you need to do is:

1. **Digitize direct instruction.** At some point soon, you'll explain something new to your students. But David might already know it, Anna might not be prepared to understand it, and Troy might not be there at all. A live explanation won't meet any of their needs.

   If you can provide that explanation on video, however, then David can fast-forward, Anna can pause to rewatch or ask you questions, and Troy can watch at home or when he returns to class. Plus, you'll never have to repeat that explanation again.

   So start a video call with yourself, hit the record button, and explain your content clearly and concisely, just like you would in class. (Or, if you prefer, find a good video online.) Congratulations! You now have a resource that your students can use to learn anytime, anywhere—and that you can reuse for the rest of your career.

2. **Get learners working together.** Watching videos is an individual activity, but learning is a social process. If your students can work together to apply the skills and concepts from your video, they'll learn more, have more fun, and become more self-sufficient too.

   So after each video, give your students something to do off-screen, and a clear place where they can do it together. Explain how collaboration benefits them, then encourage them to seek help from one another whenever they need it. Once your students can support each other, everyone's life becomes easier.

3. **Sit down with your students.** When you don't need to deliver direct instruction live, you're free to spend class working closely

with students. You can connect with students one-on-one, then deliver small-group mini-lessons when several students need the same support. At the start and/or end of class, you can also use whole-class instruction to build community, review big ideas, or facilitate special activities.

However you spend your time, make sure to check in with each of your learners regularly. Every student deserves your attention and encouragement! I bet you'll enjoy these interactions, and I know your learners will too.

4. **Require mastery.** Your goal is to help your students understand new things. So when students are ready, give them the chance to show what they know! You can adapt a simple Mastery Check template like the one I shared in Part 1, or use assessment questions you already have.

When students demonstrate mastery, let them move on. And when students fall short, help them revise until they are ready to try again. That way, students won't advance until they are actually prepared to succeed.

At its core, this is all a Modern Classroom lesson really requires: a video (or other digital direct instruction), collaborative practice, support from you, and a Mastery Check to ensure that students truly understand. If you have a lesson in mind, you can plan those components right away.

And don't worry about making any of this perfect! Nothing ever is. Plus, you'll get faster and more confident every day. But you can't start improving until you get started.

TEACHER TIP

LISA DEWITT, MIDDLE SCHOOL MATH & SCIENCE TEACHER (ROCKFORD, MICHIGAN)

"It's okay to start small. If you teach more than one content area or course, try implementing in just one of them. Start replacing lectures with instructional videos and guided notes as a first step, then focus on mastery by breaking down your standards and developing short assessments. It doesn't have to be an all-or-none situation when you're just starting out: whatever you do, you and your students are still going to see benefits."

Modernize Your Course(s)

Each of your Modern Classroom lessons will help your students master something new. To help each learner master as much as they can, while covering your course's essential content, you can combine those individual lessons into a cohesive self-paced course.

To redesign your course(s):

5. **Help learners set the pace.** You want to give students autonomy, but you don't want the gaps between them to grow too wide. So consult your calendar and decide how long you'll let learners pace themselves before starting fresh again. A few days at a time is a good starting place.

   Then, within each of your self-paced intervals, decide which content all students truly need to know (Must-Do), what's helpful but not essential (Should-Do), and what extension activities can push advanced students even further (Aspire-to-Do). This will keep every learner appropriately challenged throughout each interval, and help you deliver appropriate support.

6. **Develop sustainable systems.** Post your content on your LMS, then make it easy to navigate. Print practice work, guided notes, and Mastery Checks, and organize them within your classroom. Then explain to your students how and where to access the things they need, and let them do it! If you're clear about your expectations, your students will rise to meet them—and your class will start to run itself.

7. **Track and communicate progress.** Create a simple chart with your students' names down the left side and the names of your lessons across the top. When students master lessons, note it on your chart, then use this data to determine how you spend class time each day.

   Once you're tracking what students understand, you can help students track their own progress too. A simple checklist and/or a whole-class progress tracker can help students identify their next steps, find partners to work with, and take well-deserved pride in achieving mastery.

8. **Inspire learners to excel.** Every student wants to succeed. In a Modern Classroom, every student can! You just need to convince them.

So invest time and energy in developing personal relationships, use incentives when helpful, and foster students' growth through regular reflection. Once they know you care about them, your students will be eager to do their best.

You aren't just teaching content here: you're preparing human beings for what lies ahead. That's hard, valuable work—the most valuable there is—and it takes time. So it's okay if your students struggle at first! Be patient, encouraging, and supportive. Over time, they'll get it.

And as your learners grow, so will you. You'll notice what systems work, and what requires adjustment. That's great! You won't get your self-paced intervals or LMS or progress trackers exactly right the first time around, but you'll refine them over time. The sooner you get started, the sooner you can improve.

TEACHER TIP

SUMALA PAIDI, K-5 STEM TEACHER (DALLAS, TEXAS)

"My advice to you is to just keep going.

"For a lot of us, this is completely different from the way that we were taught how to be teachers. I also know for a lot of us this is really different from the way we were taught as students. This is a new way of teaching, but it is very rewarding, and it is doing what is best for kids.

"It's definitely not going to be perfect the first day, and it really shouldn't be. You'll need to tweak and adjust and make revisions, every single unit if not every single day. And that is okay. None of us were perfect on day one, I promise you. And you're not in this alone. Just keep it up, and you'll do wonderfully."

Modernize Instruction

Your Modern Classroom will succeed only if your students buy in. It will be even more successful if their families and administrators do too. And if you can get your colleagues on board, you can transform instruction in your community and beyond.

To achieve this, you can:

9. **Prepare for launch.** Identify an upcoming unit and plan a few lessons in advance, along with a self-paced orientation that

shows students how to succeed. Then go for it! Your first few lessons won't be perfect, but you'll learn a lot. And I guarantee that implementing this model will get easier over time.

10. **Build buy-in.** Modern Classrooms don't just benefit teachers: they help students grow as people, let families engage deeply with instruction, and give administrators valuable data on what students truly understand. So let these stakeholders know! They may be skeptical at first, but ultimately they'll all benefit. Their insights can help you do better too.

11. **Empower your colleagues (Should-Do).** Your colleagues may teach different courses and have different styles, but the beauty of this approach is that every teacher can make it their own. So show them what you're doing, explain why, and answer their questions. Before long, you might see Modern Classrooms throughout your community.

    And remember—this helps you too! Every time someone you know adapts your practices, you have the chance to learn and improve. You can support your colleagues, and they can support you. One day I hope to learn from you as well.

12. **Shape the conversation (Aspire-to-Do).** As a teacher, you know better than anyone what your students need to succeed. So speak up! Whether it's teacher autonomy, equitable grading policies, mastery-based promotion, or anything else you believe in, I hope you'll advocate for it. The world needs more teacher-driven policies.

If you can take these steps, you can help redesign instruction. You'll be happier, your students will be more engaged, and the future of your community will be brighter.

There's just one more thing I ask:

13. **Make this approach better!** The Modern Classroom model is constantly evolving. Every day new research, technological advances, and insights from educators worldwide help MCP and its community provide better guidance and support for teachers and students alike.

    The core elements of our model have remained the same since Kareem and I taught at Eastern. But there's always more to learn, and endless room to innovate. I'm sure there are countless ways to improve the practices I've shared here, and I'm counting on you to find them.

So take what I've written here, make it your own, and do things I can't yet imagine! I can't wait to see how you make Modern Classrooms better.

Can you do all this? Why not? You're an educator, just like I was. You have different experiences and perspectives than I do, which can only help you go further. You've got a global community behind you. And if you became an educator in the first place, then I know you're not afraid of a challenge!

Thousands of Modern Classroom educators meet their learners' needs every day. You can too.

TEACHER TIP

KATIE FATIGA, MIDDLE SCHOOL SOCIAL STUDIES TEACHER (FREDERICKSBURG, VIRGINIA)

"My suggestion would just be to try.

"If you've come here because you're struggling with some aspects of teaching, this is a game changer—not only for your students but also for yourself.

"I think that when I discovered Modern Classrooms, I was in a place where I didn't know how long I could continue teaching. But now I feel like with the tools that I've gathered, through implementing my own Modern Classroom and tweaking it to make it the best that I can make it for my students, it really has made a difference for all of us. My students know what they should be doing, and they feel successful doing it, which is a great stride forward for all of them.

"This is especially true in a history classroom, where students learn about people throughout time who have controlled their own destinies. It's time for them to take control of their own destinies and for you to take control of yours. So find what you think would work best for you and for your students, and give it a try!"

It's Time to Redesign Instruction

Ten years from the day I am writing this, my sons Joshua and Simon will be in high school. I don't know today who either of them will become. They may find school easy, like David. They may struggle, like Anna. They may miss class, like Troy. More likely they—like me, and I imagine like you too—will be a mix of all three. They'll excel in some classes, falter in others, and have to miss school from time to time.

They will, in other words, have their own unique needs—just like everyone else.

And while I don't yet know who Joshua or Simon will become, I do know what I want their educations to provide. I want my children to experience instruction that challenges them when they are ahead, supports them when they are behind, and helps them catch up when they miss a day. I want them to spend their days working closely with their classmates, and learning from teachers who know and value them as human beings. I want them to use technology as a tool that facilitates interpersonal connection. And I want them to leave school every day knowing that, if they apply themselves, there will be no limit to what they can achieve.

So I'm not sharing the Modern Classroom model only as a solution for low-performing schools like Eastern or high-performing ones like Leysin American School in Switzerland. I ask you to consider implementing it because it addresses the fundamental challenge of teaching—no matter who you are or what you teach. It's what I want for my own children, and what both research and my experience suggest will be best for other children too.

I do mean what I said on this book's first page: if you think something in this book won't work for you or your students, you're probably right. So take what you like and forget the rest. You're a fellow educator, and I trust you.

But if you agree with me that a Modern Classroom can meet your learners' diverse needs, then I want to welcome you, and tell you that you're in for an amazing ride. You'll work hard, especially at the beginning, but it will get easier, and in the long run it will save you time and stress. You'll build new skills and discover new things about yourself and your students. Once you're up and running, I'm confident you'll enjoy teaching more than ever before.

And you can get started the moment you close this book.

MASTERY CHECK

This book began with three learning objectives. Before you close it, please make sure you understand how to:

☐ Explain why traditional instruction fails to meet many learners' needs.

☐ Use research-backed teaching practices to keep every student appropriately challenged—and appropriately supported—every day.

☐ Lead other educators in creating classrooms where all students can succeed.

If you're ready to meet every learner's needs, take a deep breath, start small, and have fun! Recognize that redesigning instruction is a process—it will take time and effort to get right. Celebrate your successes, be honest about your struggles, and if possible share them both with a colleague (or several). Reflect, refine, repeat. You'll get there.

Tomorrow thousands of educators will walk into their own Modern Classrooms, with their heads held high, and they will use the practices I've described in this book to ensure that every young person they serve truly learns. Their students will move at different paces, and some will need multiple attempts to reach mastery. (That's learning.) And yes, these educators will work hard. (That's teaching.) But at the end of each day, these educators will go home knowing they've done the best they can to meet every learner's needs.

I hope you'll join them.

Notes on Research

When I first developed my approach to instruction, I didn't have much time to read the research on teaching. To be honest, I was just trying to get it through each day without feeling like a failure.

Since co-founding MCP, however, I've spent many enjoyable days researching the science of learning, then using insights from this academic literature to refine the Modern Classroom model. MCP has commissioned several literature reviews, and I've spoken with a wide range of experts on ways in which this research can support our teachers' practice.

For readers interested in learning more—which I recommend!—I can share a few studies that have significantly shaped the design and implementation of the Modern Classroom model.

REFERENCE	DESCRIPTION
Anderson, S.A. (1994). Synthesis of research on mastery learning. Information Analyses (ERIC Reproduction ED 382 567) Kulik, C., Kulik, J., & Bangert-Drowns, R. (1990). Effectiveness of mastery learning programs: A meta-analysis. Review of Educational Research, 60(2), 265–299. Guskey, T.R., 2015. Mastery Learning. International Encyclopedia of the Social & Behavioral Sciences, 2nd edition, Vol 14. Oxford: Elsevier. pp. 752–759.	The ideas behind mastery-based learning aren't new; in fact, they have been comprehensively studied for decades. These literature reviews summarize the many benefits of mastery learning, including but not limited to greater student satisfaction and more positive attitudes toward learning, improved academic self-concept, decreased variability in aptitude between students, and enhanced ability for students to retain learning long-term.

Reference	Description
Brame, C.J. Effective Educational Videos: Principles and Guidelines for Maximizing Student Learning from Video Content. CBE Life Sci Educ. 2016 Winter; 15(4).	This detailed review of the research on instructional videos informs the guidance I provide on effective digital direct instruction. In particular, this article explains the importance of weeding (removing irrelevant content), segmenting (chunking information with natural pauses), and signaling (using visual clues to highlight key information) to reduce students' cognitive loads. It also provides useful guidance on video length, interactivity, tone, and tempo. The techniques described here are what bring digital direct instruction in Modern Classrooms to life.
Cronin-Golomb, L. M., & Bauer, P. J. (2023). Self-motivated and directed learning across the lifespan. Acta Psychologica, 232, 1–15.	Perhaps the greatest differentiator of the Modern Classroom model—and at the same time one of its greatest benefits to students—is the autonomy it provides students to control their own learning. This review of the literature emphasizes the benefits of this approach for learners while highlighting several factors that can help learners succeed in self-motivated learning environments. Its findings inform much of my advice on supporting self-paced learning.
Marzano, R.J., Pickering, D.J., & Pollack, J.E. (2001). Classroom instruction that works: Research-based strategies for increasing student achievement. Alexandria, VA: ASCD and McREL Marzano, R.J. (2007). The art and science of teaching: A comprehensive framework for effective instruction. Alexandria, VA: Association for Supervision and Curriculum Development (ASCD).	Dr. Marzano's work highlights the importance of several practices which are central to the Modern Classroom model: note-taking during videos, focused and deliberate practice, providing immediate feedback on student work, breaking complex content into manageable chunks, metacognitive reflection, and progress tracking by students and teachers alike.

REFERENCE	DESCRIPTION
National Research Council. (2000). How people learn: Brain, mind, experience, and school (Expanded ed.). Washington, DC: National Academy Press.	This comprehensive review of research on the science of learning highlights the importance of several practices at the core of the Modern Classroom model. In particular, this science emphasizes the importance of mastery, the value of metacognition, and the benefits students experience when they take control of their own learning. The "learner-centered" approach the authors recommend, like the Modern Classroom model, places each student's individual needs at the forefront of instruction.
Reilly, J.M. (2020). The Modern Classrooms Project: A review of research-based best practices. Baltimore, MD: Johns Hopkins University.	Early in its development, MCP contracted with the Center for Research and Reform in Education at Johns Hopkins University to perform a comprehensive review of the literature on self-paced, mastery-based learning. This review highlights best practices based on decades of academic research, many of which are now deeply embedded in the model I've described in this book.
Topping, K. J., Douglas, W., Robertson, D., & Ferguson, N. (2022). Effectiveness of online and blended learning from schools: A systematic review. Review of Education, 10.	This recent meta-analysis reviewed over 1,000 studies of digital instruction and concluded that, overall, digital instruction was more effective than regular instruction in 85% of studies. Of the strategies reviewed, blended learning—a style of instruction that combines digital media with face-to-face teaching—was found to be particularly effective.

In addition to this background research, MCP contracted with the Center for Research and Reform in Education at Johns Hopkins University from 2018 to 2021 to perform independent analyses of survey data from Modern Classroom teachers and students. These analyses demonstrated the impacts of the Modern Classroom model and suggested areas for improvement, many of which I have incorporated into my description of our approach. The relevant studies, each of which I recommend reading in full, are:

◆ Wolf, B. (2019). Survey Findings for 2018–19 Implementation of The Modern Classrooms Project. Baltimore, MD: Johns Hopkins University.

◆ Wolf, B., Eisinger, J., & Ross, S. (2020). The Modern Classrooms Project: Survey Results for the 2019–20 School Year. Baltimore, MD: Johns Hopkins University.

◆ Morrison, J.R., Cook, M.A., Eisinger, J., & Ross, S.M. (2021). The Modern Classrooms Project: Evaluation Results for the 2020–21 School Year. Baltimore, MD: Johns Hopkins University.

This listing is in no way comprehensive: there's a lot more out there, and MCP learns new things—and conducts new research—about this approach all the time. But for a deeper dive into the research behind the Modern Classroom model at the time of this writing, these resources provide an excellent start.

And to explore MCP's latest program-impact research, please visit www.modernclassrooms.org.

Notes on Teacher Tips

The hardest part of writing this book was choosing which teachers' tips to feature. As of September 2024, MCP has certified more than 1,000 Distinguished Modern Classroom Educators worldwide, each of whom has demonstrated their effective implementation of our model and each of whom has wisdom worth sharing. I have visited many of these educators' classrooms myself, reviewed many more of their materials, and learned from every one of them. Many of these educators also now serve as Expert Modern Classroom Mentors, whom MCP pays to train teachers and administrators around the world.

While I did my best to include a representative sample of the incredibly diverse educators whom MCP has empowered, I realize that what I've shared here is only a small fraction of the classroom-tested wisdom that the larger Modern Classroom community has to share.

To learn more about how educators worldwide use Modern Classroom practices in the specific grade levels and content areas they teach—and to access resources these educators use every day—I recommend you:

- ◆ **Explore teacher-created materials.** At www.meeteverylearnersneeds.org, you'll find sample lesson plans, video walk-throughs of Modern Classrooms, content- and grade-level-specific guidance, articles written by Modern Classroom educators, and teacher-created templates you can copy and adapt for your own students. These resources are updated regularly and—like the Modern Classroom model itself—will continue to evolve.

- ◆ **Join MCP's online communities and events.** As of September 2024, MCP maintains an active Facebook Group with more than 20,000 members worldwide, and hosts regular virtual events where educators can connect, discover new tools and techniques, and share their struggles and successes.[1] I've learned a great deal from the MCP community, and I'm confident you will too.

---

[1] As of September 2024, you can access the Facebook group at www. facebook.com/groups/modernclassrooms, and you can access events through MCP's website (www.modernclassrooms.org).

◆ **Connect with an expert.** This book contains all the guidance you'll need to launch and lead your own Modern Classroom. But if you have questions, encounter challenges, or just want a thought partner, a conversation with an expert Modern Classroom educator can provide invaluable advice and encouragement. Visit www.meeteverylearnersneeds.org to learn more.

Teachers helping each other succeed—that's what the Modern Classroom movement is all about.

Index

Note: Page references in *italics* refer to figures and tables.